bibliography
of food consumption surveys

statistics division
economic and social policy department

FOOD AND AGRICULTURE ORGANIZATION OF THE UNITED NATIONS
Rome 1981

The designations employed and the presentation
of material in this publication do not imply the
expression of any opinion whatsoever on the
part of the Food and Agriculture Organization
of the United Nations concerning the legal
status of any country, territory, city or area or
of its authorities, or concerning the delimitation
of its frontiers or boundaries.

M-87

ISBN 92-5-101040-4

TABLE OF CONTENTS

BIBLIOGRAPHY OF FOOD CONSUMPTION SURVEYS

FOREWORD

During the past decade, government agencies and their planning services have felt the need for including food consumption and the associated factors as integral parts of their national economic and social development planning. The analysis of levels and standards of living, considered both from the angle of a description of the current situation and of the medium or long-term perspective, provides valuable guidance in national policy making and programme formulation.

At the international level too, it has been found important to analyse such information from countries so that a world picture can be drawn up as a basis for the formulation of international policies designed to improve the world food and nutrition situation and reduce the imbalances in dietary standards between countries. The 19th FAO Conference, held in Rome in 1977, attached great importance to such policies and programmes aimed at improving nutrition. It further stressed the need for better data on the food and nutrition situation of countries and recommended that assessments such as the Fourth World Food Survey be kept as up to date as possible. Work has already been started to broaden and improve the data base with respect to food consumption and related topics, with a view to publish the Fifth World Food Survey in 1984/85.

Food consumption surveys are the main sources of information required to meet the objectives stipulated above. They furnish data for the measurement of variations in consumption of all food and particular foods by source, by season, with consumer characteristics and among geographical areas. Furthermore, they provide a useful basis for measuring the relationship between the variations in patterns of food consumed and nutrient supplies on the one hand, and between variations in food consumption, food intake, nutritional intake and demographic, socio-economic, cultural, environmental and institutional factors and conditions, on the other.

Although a wide range of data on household budget and food consumption surveys has been made available, its use has been much limited because the coverage of the surveys conducted has been restricted to certain geographical areas or socio-economic groups of the population; moreover, many of these surveys have not provided sufficient information on quantities of food consumed for analysis against the relevant socio-economic variables. More importantly, the results of these surveys have not always been available to a wide range of research workers outside the countries in which the surveys have been undertaken.

The purpose of this bibliography is therefore to catalogue, as briefly as possible, some of the main features of the content and results of recent household budget and food consumption surveys conducted in different countries. The surveys covered are those conducted from 1968 to 1978 and the information is obtained from reports of these surveys available in FAO. The objective is to present, in a single publication, the sources of this information, so as to facilitate the procurement of the requisite copies or information from national statistical offices or other organizations responsible for the surveys.

Methodological and tabulated results of some of the surveys listed in this bibliography have already been presented in various issues of the Review of Food Consumption Surveys, FAO, Rome, 1958, 1962, 1970 and 1977. But the main purpose of the bibliography is to further improve the coverage and include many other subejcts for which information is available, in addition to that presented in the above Reviews. Adequate cross-referencing with the Reviews has been made in order to direct readers to the more detailed methodological and statistical texts of some of these surveys.

The bibliography is divided into two parts:

Part I consists of a list, by regions and country, of household budget and food consumption surveys, giving the source of the publication. This is followed by a short note on the general content of the survey report mainly in terms of the main objectives of the survey, the period when it was undertaken, the general scope and coverage of the survey and the main features of statistical results contained in these reports.

Part II consists of a summary table listing the surveys in the same order as in Part I, but giving their content in as systematic and comparable manner as possible. The summary table covers some details of the type of survey and the year in which it was undertaken; the over-all coverage of the surveys (in terms of geographical areas and of the socio-economic groups of the population), the sample size, the duration of the survey, the reporting period used, and the nature of results available from the surveys. The final part of the table presents some details of the tabulated and analytical results of the survey available in this report.

This bibliography is prepared to update the previous bibliographies of food consumption surveys published by FAO in 1964, 1965, 1967 and 1973. The production of this document has been made possible through the countries own efforts in providing FAO with the reports of their food consumption surveys. Its preparation has been facilitated by the new cataloguing methods adopted in the FAO Main Library, that summarise the contents of the published reports of these surveys which have now been stored in one place.

Although the bibliography has been prepared as carefully as possible, there may be certain errors in the information furnished. It is hoped that readers of this report will help to correct these errors, supply any additional details that may be necessary and continue to furnish FAO with the results of household budget and food consumption surveys that may be available in the countries. All such material should be sent to the Director, Statistics Division, FAO, Rome.

PART I

BRIEF DESCRIPTION OF SURVEY AND CONTENT OF REPORT

A F R I C A

Republique Algérienne Démocratique et Populaire
Ministère de l'Agriculture et de la Révolution Agraire
Rapport sur la Situation Alimentaire en Algérie
Direction des Etudes et de la Planification
Avril 1979 - 59 pp. in French

The report presents methodological information and results of a food consumption
survey carried out by the Ministry of Agriculture in rural areas of the northern part
of the country during the period January 1976 to January 1977. This survey was one of
several undertaken by the Ministry of Agriculture and Agrarian Reform aimed at assessing
the situation of agriculture which is the country's main resource. In particular, the
objective of this study was to collect data on actual food consumption (including measurement of consumption of own-produced food). Data reported refer to food consumed per
person during various periods of the year and by different types of agricultural workers.

Republic of Botswana
Ministry of Finance and Development Planning
Central Statistical Office
Household Expenditure Survey 1968-70
The Government Printer, Gaborone
30 pp. in English

The objective of the survey was to provide the weights for a Botswana cost of
living index and to study household expenditure patterns so as to have a benchmark on
the cash purchases of households and some rough checks on private consumption expenditure
in the monetary sector of the economy. The report contains some information on the
methodology of the survey, e.g., sample design, coverage, methods of enumeration and some
tables on food and other household expenditures by three main income classes and geographical areas.

See: Review of Food Consumption Surveys, Vol. II, FAO, Rome; pp. 22 and 23 for a detailed
description of the scope and methods of the survey.

Republique du Burundi
Ministère du Plan - Division de la Statistique
et Republique Française
Ministère des Affaires Etrangères
Coopération Technique
Enquête Statistique Alimentaire et Budgetaire 1970-71 dans la Région Ngozi et Muyinga
Rapport et Annexes; 170 and 241 pp. in French
SEDS Paris, Mars, 1973

The objectives of the enquiry, which was carried out during the period August 1970 - July 1971 were, from the point of view of consumption, to measure the quantity, value and nutritive quality of food consumption and to establish its origin; from the points of view of household budget, to study the distribution of expenditures and source of income. The report is divided into 3 parts; Part 1 gives a brief description of the country and its agriculture and general information of the survey methodology used. Parts 2 and 3 deal more specifically with the food consumption and budgetary enquiries.

The volume of annexes contains tables presenting data relating to the consumption and budget parts of the enquiry, e.g., nutrition value of the diet, prices, source of income and expenditure by various characteristics of the head of the household and expenditure by income groups, including expenditure on total food. The Annex to Volume 2 contains the facsimile of the questionnaires used.

Republique du Burundi
Département des Etudes et Statistiques
Enquête aupres des Ménages de Bujumbura 1978-79
Bulletin Statistique Août 1979
58 pp. in French, plus annexes comprising questionnaires and tables

The survey was considered as a first step in the establishment of a system of household enquiries. The objective of the survey was to collect data for updating the cost of living index and for studying the levels of living of households. It was carried out during the period September 1978 to August 1979. The report contains a methodological summary dealing with the sample design, organization of fieldwork, calendar of operations etc., and results of the pilot survey. These results relate to the socio-economic and demographic characteristics of the sample and to household average expenditures by household size and by city areas. It includes a facsimile of the questionnaire used.

République du Tchad
Ministère du Plan et de la Coopération
Sous-Direction de la Statistique
Enquête Budget-Consommation à N'Djamena 1972 (Fort-Lamy)
45 pp. in French

The objective of the survey was to study the distribution of household expenditure and to provide data for use in compiling the weights for a consumer price index for salaried population with low incomes. The report gives a brief description of the methodology of the enquiry, which was carried out amongst families of the capital Fort-Lamy from November 1971 to November 1972. It also presents a series of tables containing data on demographic characteristics of the households, household cash income, expenditure, including food, by income group.

See: Review of Food Consumption Surveys, 1977, Vol. II, FAO, Rome; pp. 35-36 for a detailed description of the scope and methods of the survey and p. 134 for the tabulated results on food expenditure.

CENTRAL AFRICA

FAO-UN Project CAF/72/011
Rapport Final par BUI QUANG MINH
Enquête Budget et Consommation des Ménages - Annex II - Resultats Statistiques,
172 pp. in French   Bangui, Juin 1977

The survey was carried out during the period 1975-76 by the Ministry of Planning, Cooperation and Statistics with the cooperation of UNDP. The results published were obtained
from the manual processing of data relating to the first cycle only. Data reported cover
the socio-demographic characteristics of the sample, living conditions, agricultural
production, cash expenditures, food consumption in terms of quantity and calorie content,
by rural/urban/forest areas and by other household characteristics.

KENYA

Ministry of Finance and Planning
Central Bureau of Statistics and
FAO Marketing Development Project
Urban Food Purchasing Survey 1977, Part 1
Nairobi
English

The objective of the survey was to collect data that would enable the analysis of the food
purchasing behaviour of certain consumers as an aid to the overall diagnostic study of
food marketing. Data in the report relate to the first phase of the Urban Survey, i.e.
April-June 1977. This Part 1 of the report is but one of a series of survey reports to
be issued by the FAO Marketing Development Project. Data on household expenditures,
including food, on household purchasing habits, on income and demographic characteristics
of households are shown for each of the four urban areas covered in the survey, namely,
Nairobi, Mombasa, Nakuru and Kisumu. A Chapter on survey design and methodology is
included together with a sample of the questionnaires used.

See: Review of Food Consumption Surveys, 1977, Vol. II, FAO, Rome; pp. 71-72 for a detailed
description of the scope and methods of the survey and pp. 194-198 for the tabulated results
on food expenditure.

LESOTHO

A.M. Monyake
Extract from the Report on the Rural Household Consumption and Expenditure Survey 1967-69
The Bureau of Statistics
Maseru, May 1973
20 pp. in English

The objective of the enquiry carried out by the Bureau of Statistics during April 1967 and
April 1969 was to establish estimates of the contribution of the rural sector to the National
Income as well as the disposal of that income. The report gives a description of the design of
the survey and a comment on the eight tables it contains, which relate to value and sources of
income and expenditures, including food, by area and income class.

See: Review of Food Consumption Surveys, 1977, Vol. II, FAO, Rome; pp. 75-76 for a detailed
description of the scope and methods of the survey and p. 203 for the tabulated results on
food expenditure.

The Bureau of Statistics
1972/73 Urban Household Budget Survey Report
Maseru, October 1973
57 pp. in English

The objective of the survey was to provide the basis for setting up Lesotho's first retail
price index and to assist in the estimation of private consumption for use in National
Accounts. It was the first urban household survey conducted in Lesotho and covered a
complete year in order to take into account seasonal variations in expenditure and income.

The report consists of a descriptive part relating to the objectives of the survey,
the methodology applied, sequence and methods of operation, and a commentary on the results.
It contains nine tables relating to demographic data, household and per capita income, income
source and household expenditure.

See: Review of Food Consumption Surveys, 1977, Vol. II, FAO, Rome; pp. 77-78 for a detailed
description of the scope and methods of the survey, p. 204 for the tabulated results on food
expenditure.

Kingdom of Lesotho
Report of the Lesotho Pilot Survey on Population and Food Consumption, May 1973
Bureau of Statistics, Maseru, January 1975
68 pp. in English

A combined study of food consumption habits with investigation of the attitudes of the
respondents to change in population and agriculture. Its purpose was to investigate the
inter-relationships between food consumption, agricultural development and population
dynamics, and to develop suitable methodology for similar surveys to be promoted in other
developing countries. It was carried out in May 1973.

The report consists of five parts; three dealing with the organization and methodology
and technical problems of the survey; and two with survey results, one of which deals
with some aspects of supply and demand for food. In the annex, instructions to enumerators
and questionnaires used are included.

MADAGASCAR

Repoblika Malagasy
Institut National de la Statistique et de la Recherche Economique
Enquête sur les Budgets des Ménages en Milieu Rural (1968/69)
(Antanifotsy - Maroantsetra - Morondava - Vohipeno)
124 pp. in French

Besides collecting data on levels of living and on family budgets in rural areas during a
period of 12 months, the enquiry had the objective of improving the methodology employed
in such surveys and of assessing the effect of external influence on the level of living
of rural population. The report consists of 4 parts, the first dealing with methodological
aspects; the second with households characteristics, including definitions and various
tables on households demographic characteristics and distribution by income, geographical
area and other demographic data; the third one with the concept of income, its source and
distribution; the fourth one with all households expenditures in cash or without cash,
including food expenditures, by income class and geographical area.

See: <u>Review of Food Consumption Surveys,</u> 1977, Vol. II, FAO Rome; pp. 206-209 for the tabulated results on food expenditure.

Repoblika Malagasy
Institut National de la Statistique et de la Recherche Economique
<u>Enquête sur les Budgets des Ménages Malgaches à Tananarive Ville*1968-69</u>
69 pp. in French

The survey covered the city of Tananarive and was conducted during a period of 12 months from March 1968 to March 1969.

The report, consisting of 3 parts, deals with the methodology employed, the concepts and definitions and the survey results, it also relates on the findings of an enquiry carried out among Malagasyan residents of Tananarive to assess their level of living. It contains data on demographic characteristics, income (value, source, nature and distribution) and expenditure including that on food.

Repoblika Malagasy
Institut National de la Statistique et de la Recherche Economique
<u>Enquête sur les Dépenses des Ménages Etrangers à Tananarive-Ville*</u> (1969)
48 pp. in French

The objective of the survey was to assess the importance of consumption of foreigners' households on the economy of the capital of Madagascar and to collect data useful for the calculation of an Index of Consumer Prices. Field work was carried out in May-June 1969.

The report follows in outline and content the other report (see "Enquête sur les Budgets des Ménages Malgaches à Tananarive Ville 1968-69") on households of Malagasyan origin only. It contains the first part describing the methodology and coverage of the survey and the second part presenting the results on households characteristics, household distribution by expenditure level and on the distribution of expenditures.

                                                                           MALAWI

Malawi Government
National Statistical Office
<u>Household Income and Expenditure Survey for Urban Areas and Agricultural Estates, 1968</u>
The Government Printer, Zomba, May 1970
259 pp. in English

The main purpose of the survey was to ascertain the income levels and the pattern of expenditure of households in the non-village areas. It was conducted between 28 January 1968 and February 1969. The report consists of a descriptive part on the methodology used, i.e. sample design, fieldwork, definition, coverage etc., and of a series of 23 tables for each survey zone (there are six) on household expenditure, including the expenditure on food, income and household characteristics. The specimen of the questionnaires used are also included in the report.

See: <u>Review of Food Consumption Surveys,</u> 1977, Vol. II, FAO, Rome; pp. 82-84 for detailed description of the scope and methods of the survey and pp. 210-216 for the tabulated results on food expenditure.

* Now Antananarivo.-

Royaume du Maroc
Secrétariat d'Etat au Plan, au Développement Régional et à la Formation des Cadres
La Consommation et les Dépenses des Ménages au Maroc 1970-1971
Division de Statistiques
Vol. I: Premiers Resultats à l'Echelon National - Avril 1972
Vol. II: Coefficients d'Elasticité - Mai 1973
Vol. IV: Alimentation et Nutrition - Juin 1973
73, 59, 181 pp. respectively in French

The main objective of the enquiry was to study the levels of living of the population
in relation to various household demographic and economic characteristics. All private
households in Morocco including those of foreigners residing there, but excluding those
belonging to the diplomatic service, were covered by the survey which lasted a period of
12 months.

The methodology employed in carrying out the enquiry, i.e. information on sample design,
characteristics of the population under study, methods of enumeration, definitions,
is outlined in Vol. I of the report together with a number of tables presenting data
on household distribution and expenditure in terms of national averages. Vols. II and IV
consist mainly of tables giving data on elasticity coefficients and on food consumption
and nutrition. A short introduction on the methods of calculation used and on the
analysis of results is included in these volumes.

See: Review of Food Consumption Surveys, 1977, Vol. II, FAO, Rome; pp. 89-90 for a detailed
description of the scope and methods of the survey and pp. 228-233 for the tabulated
results on food consumption.

REUNION

G. Le Cointre
Enquête sur les Revenus et Dépenses des Ménages de la Réunion 1976-77
Service Départemental de Statistique de La Réunion
Etudes no. 11 - INSEE - Dec. 1978
166 pp. in French plus annex

The survey covered the whole territory of Reunion and all types of private households,
in rural and urban areas, during the period April 1976 to April 1977. The objective
of the enquiry was to study income and expenditure patterns of households.

The report contains methodological information on the conduct of the survey and an analysis
of principal results, specifically those on income and expenditure and their variation
according to dwelling place, household size, number of active household members and
the socio-economic category of household head. In the annex tables is presented the
data on distribution of households and of households income and expenditure.

RWANDA

H. L. Vis, C. Yourassowsky, H. Van der Borght
Une enquête de Consommation Alimentaire en République Rwandaise
Institut National de Recherche Scientifique
Publication n. 10 - Butare, Rwanda - 1972
187 pp. in French

This food consumption survey was carried out over the whole national territory of Rwanda
during the years 1966-1972.

It was a combined food consumption and nutrition survey; and scales of nutrition requirements
and the levels of food intakes were established particularly for rural areas.

The report contains information on the demographic characteristics of the population, a description of the food consumption survey methodology and of the method used in establishing nutritive requirements. It contains an analysis of results obtained including data on the food consumption (quantity and nutritive value) of municipalities.

SENEGAL

Université de Dakar
Institut Universitaire de Technologie
Etude: Budget Consommation
II Enquête: Budgets Familiaux
June 1976; around 200 pp. in French

The survey covered only African households in the city of Dakar during the period 24 February - 23 March 1975. Its main objective was to study income and expenditure patterns, of households in relation to well defined socio-economic criteria. The study enquired into social and demographic characteristics of households, household and individual expenditures, gift received and given away and into expenditure on durable goods.

The report presents information on the survey methodology as well as on the analysis of results obtained by each of the characteristics studied. A facsimile of questionnaires used is included in the report.

SIERRA LEONE

Central Statistical Office
Household Survey 1966-1970
Freetown 1970-72
Several reports on Household Characteristics and Housing Conditions and on Household Expenditure and Income and Economic Characteristics for Eastern, Western, Southern and Northern Province, separately for urban and rural areas.
Around 100 pp. each in English

This multipurpose survey was intended to provide information on household characteristics, housing conditions, expenditure patterns and other data relating to the household sector of the economy. It was a nation-wide survey covering the various provinces and the urban and rural areas. These were surveyed at different times between the years 1968 and 1970.

The various reports contain, as specified in the title, data on household characteristics, housing conditions and on household income and expenditure. All reports consist of a descriptive part covering the methodology of the survey, i.e. sample design, enumeration, definitions, etc. and a tabular part consisting mainly of statistical tables presenting data on topics mentioned above including some data on quantity of food consumed.

See: Review of Food Consumption Surveys, 1977, Vol. II, FAO, Rome; pp. 95-96 for a detailed description of the scope and methods of the survey and pp. 261-264 for the tabulated results on food expenditure.

Somali Democratic Republic
Mogadishu Family Budget Survey 1977
Central Statistical Department
Mogadishu 1978
49 pp. in Somali and English

The survey was undertaken with the purpose of collecting data useful for revising the Consumer Price Index and other data on household demographic characteristics, expenditure and income. It covered a sample of private Somali households living within the urban limits of Mogadishu, and was undertaken in four rounds, starting from March 1977 through December 1977.

The report, besides containing some information on the survey methodology, presents data on the distribution of households and expenditure by certain household characteristics such as size and total expenditure.

A facsimile of the questionnaire used is included in the report.

Republic of South Africa, Department of Statistics
Survey of Household Expenditure 1975
Report 11-06-05
The Government Printer, Pretoria - March 1979
315 pp. (English and Dutch)

The report contains detailed results of the sample survey of expenditure of white households which was undertaken in the principal urban areas of the Republic, during October and November 1975. The objective of the survey was to determine average expenditure patterns for the calculation of the Consumer Price Index. Some information on sample design and coverage is provided in the report. In addition to the data on average expenditure patterns, the report also contains information on income, dwellings and on household composition.

Bureau of Statistics
Ministry of Economic Affairs and Development Planning
1969 Household Budget Survey
Vol. I: Income and Consumption - 223 pp. (Eglish)
Vol. II: Housing Conditions - 82 pp. (English)
Vol. III: Retail Prices - 9 pp. plus appendices (English)
Dar-Es-Salaam 1972 for Vol. I and III, 1971 for Vol. II

The main purpose of the survey was to measure the levels of living of the population in different areas of the country and in different income groups and also to estimate the aggregate private consumption expenditure required for national accounts and to estimate future demand for selected items of consumption, to obtain weights for a consumer price index. The survey was the first country-wide and year-long household budget survey in Tanzania. It covered the full calendar year 1969.

Vol. I of the report of this Survey deals with income, consumption and expenditure of private households. This volume also contains some methodological information on the conduct of the survey. Vol. II deals with housing conditions and Vol. III with retail prices. All information is available separately for urban and rural areas and for the Tanzania mainland.

See: Review of Food Cosnumption Surveys, 1977, Vol. II, FAO, Rome; pp. 97-99 for a detailed description of the scope and methods of the survey and pp. 269-271 for the tabulated results on food expenditure.

TUNISIA

Ministère du Plan
Institut National de la Statistique
Enquête Nationale sur le Budget et la Consommation des Ménages 1975
Tunis, Avril 1978
500 pp. in French

This nation-wide survey, covering both rural and urban areas of the country was the second of the major surveys to be carried out in the country. The objectives of this survey were, inter alia: to study the family budget structure by different variables, such as income, social groups, demographic characteristics etc.; to extract new coefficients for the index of consumer prices; to analyze household demand for food products and to assess the nutritional status of the population.

The report consists of three parts. The first part deals with the methodology of the survey, including objectives, survey design, methods of enumeration and organization of the survey. The second part consists of a study of household expenditure distribution, and an analysis of the household budgets and household expenditure behaviour. The third part analyzes the household food consumption and its nutritional content, in relation to requirements.

A facsimile of the questionnaires used is also included in the report.

ZAIRE

Republique du Zaïre
Institut National de la Statistique
Etudes Statistiques
Rapport sur l'Enquête des Budgets Familiaux en Milieu Africain, Ville de Bukavu (Sept.1971)
Kinshasa, June 1973

The Survey was meant to study the living conditions of the population in the city of Bukavu. The survey lasted one month and covered two percent of the total population. The major interest of this survey lay in the effort deployed to improve the methodology and on the variety of results (food, health, education, employment etc.). The report consists of seven parts relating respectively to: presentation of the survey; introduction; methodology; analysis of data on population, housing, food expenditure and consumption, income elasticity coefficient of total and food consumption; conclusions; bibliography and various annexes including the questionnaires.

See: <u>Review of Food Consumption Surveys</u>, 1977, Vol. II, FAO, Rome; pp. 110-111 for a detailed description of the scope and methods of the survey and pp. 285 for the tabulated results on food consumption.

J. Houyoux
Université Catholique de Louvain
<u>Budgets Ménagers, Nutrition et Mode de Vie à Kinshasa</u>
Presses Universitaires du Zaïre
Kinshasa 1973
300 pp. in French

The objective of the survey was to study the levels of living and consumption habits of the urban population. It covered all types of African households in Kinshasa during a year so that seasonal variation in consumption could be studied.

The report reviews the demographic changes and workers' remuneration in the city of Kinshasa, before presenting data on household food expenditure in relation to economic level, socio-professional category, dwelling place and education. The study was used as a base for calculating a new consumer price index which (since May 1975) is calculated every month.

See: <u>Review of Food Consumption Surveys</u>, 1977, Vol. II, FAO, Rome; pp. 108-109 for a detailed description of the scope and methods of the survey and pp. 284 for the tabulated results on food expenditure.

M. Cresta e R. Mazzoni
<u>Indagine sull'Alimentazione e la Nutrizione di Mbanza - Ngungu svolta nel quadro di un progetto integrato di studio agro-socio-economico interessante l'ovest dello Zaire, 1975</u>
Report received 26.9.78
70 typewritten pp. plus annexes in Italian

The survey was aimed at determining the food needs of the rural population. To this end, the relationships existing among food consumption, nutrition needs, demographic characteristics, employment and income were studied. The survey covered both urban and rural households in the region during May 1975. Part I of the report describes the survey methodolgy; demographic characteristics and habitat of the population under study; distribution of rural and urban population; food intake and expenditure; analysis of the influence of number of children and economic conditions. Part II consists of tables presenting all data collected on food consumption, nutrition and expenditure, separately for rural and urban households in the region.

ZIMBAWE

Central Statistical Office
1. Report on Urban African Budget Survey in Bulawayo 1968
2. Report on Urban African Budget Survey in Salisbury, 1969
3. Report on the European Family Budget Survey in Salisbury 1969/71
4. Report on the Urban African Budget Survey in the Midlands (Gwelo, Que Que and Gatooma), 1970
5. Report on the Urban African Budget Survey in Umtali, 1971
6. European Expenditure Survey 1975/76
Salisbury, Zimbawe
July 1970 - April 1978
19 to 39 pp. each

The above surveys were held mainly for the purpose of reviewing the weighting structure
used in calculating the Consumer Price Index.

The time coverage of the various surveys was as follows: 1) 1 November to 5 December 1968;
2) 26 September - 5 December 1969; 3) 3 year period 1969-1971; 4) 26 September - 5 December
1970; 5) 26 September - 5 December 1971; 6) January 1975 - December 1976..

Each report consists of a short descriptive part indicating the survey's coverage, sampling
methods, level of response, duration, fieldwork costs, and of a set of tables showing
data on household size, composition, standard of education, income, source of income
and expenditures including food expenditures; also some data on quantity of food consumed
are included.

AFRICA (SEDES)

République Française
Secrétariat d'Etat aux Affaires Etrangères
L'Approvisionnement des Villes dans les Pays Francophones d'Afrique
Enquêtes et Perspectives
Vol. I - Rapport de Synthese-Enquête Economique auprès des Familles
Vol. II - Abidjan - Bouaké (Ivory Coast)
Vol. III - Lomé (Togo)
Vol. IV - Ouagadougou (Upper Volta)
Vol. V - Bamako (Mali)
SEDES, Paris, December 1972 (French)

The objective of the study was to try to define the urban consumption and supply of
food products, in particular wheat, sugar and milk. Data from 16 budget and consumption
surveys carried out in the African Urban centres studied (Abidjan, Lomé, Ouagadougou,
Bamako and Bouaké) were utilized. Vol. I contains general information on food habits
and on previous (1957-65) consumption surveys carried out in the area. Vol. II contains
data on supply, distribution and consumption foods in the cities of Abidjan and Bouaké
(Ivory Coast); Lomé (Togo); Ouagadougou (Upper Volta) and Bamako (Mali).

LATIN AMERICA AND CARIBBEAN ISLANDS

Commonwealth of the Bahamas
Department of Statistics
Household Budgetary Survey Report 1970
Nassau, Bahamas 1972
20 pp. plus appendices (around 70 pp.) in English

The objective of this survey was to collect information on domestic commodities and services purchased by households to determine levels of consumer expenditure and to calculate weights for a revised index of cost of living. The survey, which took place in 1970, covered private Bahamian households of at least two persons in New Providence with incomes ranging from 3,500 to 15,000 Bahamian dollars per annum. The report presents methodological information regarding the carrying out of the survey, as well as data on daily expenditure, longer term expenditure, consumer durable expenditure as well as the summary of total expenditure per family per week.

A facsimile of the questionnaire used is included in the report.

See: Review of Food Consumption Surveys, 1977, Vol.II, FAO, Rome; pp. 20-21 for a detailed description of the scope and methods of the survey.

Commonwealth of the Bahamas
Department of Statistics
Household Expenditure in the Bahamas 1973
Nassau, Bahamas - June 1975
98 pp. in English

This was the first National Household Expenditure Survey conducted in the Bahamas. Data were to be used for calculating the official national income estimates. The report contains estimates of household expenditure by various household socio-demographic characteristics.

The National Food and Nutrition Survey of Barbados
Undertaken by the Government of Barbados with the assistance of the Caribbean Food and Nutrition Institute, the PAHO and the FAO, Washington 1972; 139 pp. (World Health Organization, Pan-American Sanitary Bureau. Scientific publication no. 237) in English

The survey, which took place in May 1969 was a joint effort of the Government of Barbados, CFNI, PAHO and FAO.

The survey was considered necessary by the Government to obtain data on food supply and nutrition on the island to be used for the planning of nutritional activities, especially the Applied Nutrition Programme. Data contained in the report refer in particular to nutrient requirements, anthropometric measurements, food economics and home garden food production.

Fundaçao Getulio Vargas
Instituto Brasileiro de Econometria
Pesquisa sobre Consumo Alimentar Oct.-Dec.1973
Vol. I-III, June 1975
From 75 up to 300 pp. in Portuguese

The Survey covered families in Rio de Janeiro living in certain types of dwellings, selected
on the basis of data supplied by COHAB (Companhia de Habitaçao Popular do Estado de Guanabara).
The variable measured was chosen as an alternative to the use of income data which were
difficult to obtain.

Report I covers survey methodology, in particular   sample design; various characteristics
of the population studied including anthropometric measurements;   households income and
expenditure; nutritive values of food consumed including comparative data on income and
nutrient intakes.

Report II covers certain aspects of the survey methodology, specifically personnel selection
and training, field organization, methods of collecting the information, coding system
and the processing of data. It includes a facsimile of the questionnaires used.

Report III covers the food consumption table of food items used and aspects of food preparation.

See: Review of Food Consumption Surveys, 1977, Vol. II, FAO, Rome; p. 30 for a detailed
description of the scope and method of the survey and pp. 127-130 for the tabulated results
on food consumption.

Fundaçao Instituto Brasileiro de Geografia e Estatística
Estudo Nacional da Despesa Familar (ENDEF)
Dados Preliminares: Consumo Alimentar-Antropometria

     (Regio 1: Estudo de Rio de Janeiro
Reports(Regio 3: Paraná, Santa Catarina, Rio Grande do Sul
     (Rio de Janeiro, IBGE, 1977 - 110 pp.

     (Regio 2: São Paulo
     (Regio 4: Minas Gerais, Espírito Santo
     (Rio de Janeiro, IBGE, 1978 - 110 pp.

     (Regio 5: Maranhão, Piauj, Ceará, Rio Grande do Norte, Paraíba, Pernambuco, Alagoas,
           Sergipe, Bahia
     (Rio de Janeiro, IBGE, 1977 - 72 pp.

     (Regio 6: Distrito Federal
     (Regio 7: Rondônia, Acre, Amazonas, Roraima, Pará, Amapá, Goiás, Mato Grosso
     (Rio de Janeiro, IBGE, 1978 - 78 pp.

Dados Preliminares: Despesas das Familias
     (Regio 5: Maranhao, Piaui, Ceará, Rio Grande do Norte, Paraíba, Pernambuco, Alagoas,
Reports   Sergipe, Bahia
     (Rio de Janeiro, IBGE, 1977 - 72 pp.

     (Regio 3: Paraná, Santa Catarina, Rio Grande do Sul
     (Rio de Janeiro, IBGE, 1977 - 99 pp.

The main objective of this survey, which covered around 55,000 families in Brazil, was to collect extensive social statistics with emphasis on food consumption and nutrition. It was carried out during the period August 1974 to August 1975. Each of the reports listed above consists of two parts: one relating to methodology used, concepts and definitions, fieldwork, methods and the other consisting of tables on average per capita food consumption, nutritive value of food consumed, household expenditure and anthropometric measurements.

See: Review of Food Consumption Surveys, 1977, Vol. II, FAO, Rome; pp. 31-32 for a detailed description of the scope and methods of the survey.

CHILE

Ministerio de Economia, Fomento y Reconstrucción
Instituto Nacional de Estadísticas
III Encuesta de Presupuestos Familiares
Diciembre 1977 - Noviembre 1978
Vol. I: Estructura del Gasto de los Hogares en el Gran Santiago, promedio anual y por trimestres
Vol. III: Estructura del Gasto de los Hogares en el Gran Santiago, por grupos quintiles de Hogares
105 pp. each in Spanish.

The survey was undertaken with the purpose of obtaining new weights for the Consumer Price Index and data relating to household income and expenditures. The survey covered the period December 1977 to November 1978. Results of the survey and the methodology used are published in different volumes. Volume 1 reports on annual and trimestrial data on average household expenditure including food, for Great Santiago. Volume III reports data on household expenditure, including food, by five household expenditure groups.

COLOMBIA

Departamento Administrativo Nacional de Estadística
Los Presupuestos Familiares en Colombia 1971
Cuarta etapa de la Encuesta Nacional de Hogares
DANE, Bogotá, Septiembre 1976
51 pp. in Spanish

The study of income and expenditure of Colombian households was the subject of the fourth stage of the Multi-purpose Household Surveys carried out on a continuous basis by DANE since 1970. The survey covers the whole national territory, and the urban and rural areas. The objectives of the survey were the study of household income and expenditure, the collection of data for the revision of the Consumer Price Index, the study of distribution of consumption and levels of living of Colombian households. The report describes the methodology of the survey and presents data on households, demographic characteristics and on average household expenditure by various characteristics, including household income. Data refer to the period June - July 1971.

Departamento Administrativo Nacional de Estadística
Ingresos y Gastos de los Hogares en Colombia
DANE, Bogotá, December 1977
92 pp. in Spanish

The National Household Survey is a continuous household multi-purpose survey carried out
by DANE since 1970. This report describes the methodology and findings of its sixth round,
the purpose of which was to collect data on income composition and distribution, on household levels of living and on the distribution of consumption. The period which the data
refer to is September - October 1972. Besides information on survey methodology including
a facsimile of the questionnaires used, data on household demographic characteristics and
on average household income and expenditures are also presented in the report.

DOMINICAN REPUBLIC

Republica Dominicana
Estudio sobre Presupuestos Familiares
Report II   Distribución del Gasto de las Familias en la Ciudad de Santo Domingo, 1969
Report IV   Indice de Precios al Consumidor en la Ciudad de Santo Domingo, 1960-1970
Report V   Consumo de Alimentos y Nutrientes en la Ciudad de Santo Domingo, 1969
Banco Central de la Republica Dominicana
Oficina Nacional de Estadistica
Agencia Internacional para el Desarrollo (USAID)
Santo Domingo, D.N. 1974

The survey, covering the city of Santo Domingo, was carried out during the period January
to December 1969, to collect data for the calculation of the cost of living index, for
determining the number of workers in each family, type of occupation, income and expenditure;
and for estimation of national accounts aggregates and demand for agricultural products.

Reports II and IV consist of tables and graphs showing data relative to the consumer price
index in Santo Domingo, for 1969 and the period 1960-1970, and of basic tables for its calculation; a couple of pages of introduction explain how the index was calculated.

Report V consists of a methodological summary, covering objectives, concepts, definitions,
sample design, organization of fieldwork, and of comments on the tables, which refer to
average per capita food consumption in terms of quantity and nutrients by food group/item,
and to household expenditure and income by family size.

See: Review of Food Consumption Surveys, 1977, Vol. II, FAO, Rome; pp. 43-44 for a detailed
description of the scope and methods of the survey and p. 140 for the tabulated results
on food expenditure.

Banco Central de la Republica Dominicana
Oficina Nacional de Estadistica
Primera Encuesta Nacional de Ingresos y Gastos de las Familias en la Republica Dominicana
Metodologia
Santo Domingo, D.N. Sept. 1976
97 pp. in Spanish

The survey was undertaken during the period May 1976 to April 1977. It had as its main
objective the collection of data for calculating a new cost of living index, assessing the
level of living of the population and their consumption habits and for studying demand of
goods and services. The present volume deals exclusively with the methodology adopted,
in particular with the survey design and sample distribution. Nineteen annexes show in
detail the sample distribution and the number of households selected.

EL SALVADOR

Dirección General de Estadistica y Censos
Ministerio de Economia, Rep. de San Salvador
Encuesta de Ingresos y Gastos Familiares 1969
(Area Metropolitana - Familias de Ingresos Menores de 600 colones)
December 1972
110 pp. in Spanish

The survey covering workers and middle class families in the Area Metropolitana of San
Salvador, comprising 9 municipalities, in the four most important cities of the country,
namely Santa Ana, San Miguel, Sonsonate, Sacatecoluca, and in ten representative rural areas
had several objectives, among which were to obtain new weights for the calculation of the
cost of living index, obtain data needed for market and demand analysis, to calculate national
expenditure etc. Besides presenting information on survey methodology, the report contains
tables with data on households demographic characteristics and on household expenditures,
including expenditure on food, by income groups and family size - for San Salvador Metropolitan
Area.

See: Review of Food Consumption Surveys, 1977, Vol. II, FAO, Rome; pp. 45-46 for a detailed
description of the scope and methods of the survey and p. 141 for the tabulated results
on food expenditure.

GUATEMALA

R. A. Orellana A. de León
Ingresos y Gastos de las Familias Urbanas de Guatemala
Instituto de Investigaciones Economicas y Sociales
Universidad de San Carlos de Guatemala
Guatemala C.A. 1972
280 pp. in Spanish

The survey covered urban families of two persons or more who had lived as one economic unit
for the whole of the preceeding year in the same town. It was carried out in the towns of
Guatemala, Esquintla, Quetzaltenango, Puerto Barrios, Jutiapa during the entire 1969. The
objective of the enquiry was to study expenditure habits relative to consumption and
services of the urban population and to collect data on quantity and value of goods and
services consumed to be used in computing a cost of living index for the urban area of
the country.

The report contains methodological information relative to the carrying out of the survey; an analysis of the survey findings and tables with data on household demographic characteristics together with their living expenditures and income.

See: Review of Food Consumption Surveys, 1977, Vol. II, FAO, Rome; pp. 53-54 for a detailed description of the scope and methods of the survey, and p. 150 for the tabulated results on food expenditure.

GUYANA

Institut National de la Statistique et des Etudes Economiques
Une Enquête sur les Consommations des Ménages dans le Département de la Guyane 1968
INSEE - Paris (received 1974)
21 pp. in French

The purpose of the survey was to collect the requisite data for preparing a Consumer Price Index. The survey covered the urban areas of Cayenne and Kouron during the months of April - June 1968 and some coastal municipalities during the months of November and December 1968.

Data reported refer to the weights calculated for the consumer price index and to the average household total monthly consumption (= expenditures).

Government of Guyana
Pan-American Health Organization
The Caribbean Food and Nutrition Institute and FAO
The National Food and Nutrition Survey of Guyana
WHO, PAN-American Sanitary Bureau
Scientific Publication No. 323 - 1976
196 pp. in English

The National Food and Nutrition Survey of Guyana was conducted from mid-April to late June 1971. It was executed through the collaborative efforts of the Government of Guyana and the Caribbean Food and Nutrition Institute. The survey covered both the urban and rural population. About 3,000 persons were covered in the anthropometric and clinical measurements taken; these also had their blood samples taken. Food consumption studies and socio-cultural and agricultural investigations were carried out on just under 1,000 families, whose household agricultural practices were also investigated. Individual food consumption was measured on a sample of 150 persons. The report covers the main survey findings and recommendations. The food consumption data included in the report are related to the recommended scales of nutrient intake and to the food balance sheets for year 1970.

HAITI

Institut Haïtien de Statistique
Département des Finances et des Affaires Economiques
Enquête Socio-Economique (Avril 1970)
Premiers Resultats
May 1975 - 60 pp. in French

The purpose of the survey was to collect a set of data on population, dwelling, family budgets, agriculture and livestock. The survey covered both urban and rural areas of the country, during the year 1970. Data reported refer to: population distribution by various characteristics such as rural/urban area, age/sex, education, etc., number of livestock, sale of agricultural products, total household expenditure. All data are also reported for rural and urban areas separately.

MEXICO

Secretaría de Industria y Comercio
Dirección General de Estadistica
Ingresos y Egresos de las Familias en la Republica Mexicana 1969-70
Tomo III, IV, V
México D.F. 1971 - 77, 85, 88 pp. respectively in Spanish

The survey was carried out over the whole national territory during the period October 1969 - March 1970 with the purpose of studying income and expenditure of the Mexican population.

Each report contains some methodological information regarding the carrying out of the survey and tables showing data on income by source, savings, expenditure and distribution of families by income group and percent of income spent on rent and by balance of income and expenditure. Data are available separately for the urban and rural areas of the federal states to which each report refers.

See: Review of Food Consumption Surveys, 1977, Vol. II, FAO, Rome; pp. 87-88 for a detailed description of the scope and methods of the survey and pp. 222-227 for the tabulated results on food expenditure.

Secretaria de Programación y Presupuesto
Coordinación General del Sistema Nacional de Información
Encuesta Nacional de Ingresos y Gastos de los Hogares 1977
Informe metodologico y Primera Observación
Mexico
246 pp. respectively, plus annex for Vol. I, in Spanish

The main purpose of the survey was to collect recent statistical data on income and expenditure of Mexican households, specially the income and expenditure structure and distribution. These data were also required for calculating new weights for the consumer price index, for the study on the level of living of Mexican households, etc. The survey covered private households living in the national territory during the first half of the survey year which was 1977.

The first report describes the methodology of the survey with the purpose of furnishing the necessary information for determining the extent and limits of the data collected during the months of August, September and the first week of October 1977 and relating to the first half of the same year.

MEXICO cont.

In the first chapter of the report, the objective, sample design and method of enumeration and processing are briefly described. In the eight subsequent chapters, details of each stage of survey taking are described in detail.

The second report contains data relating to the same period, specifically they refer to households social and demographic characteristics and to current income and expenditure. The Annex to the first report contains a facsimile of the questionnaire used.

PANAMA

Contraloria General de la Republica
Dirección de Estadistica y Censo
Estudio sobre las Condiciones de Vida de las Familias - Ciudades de Panama y Colón -
Encuesta de 1972
Estadistica Panameña, año XXXV Serie G.1 - 1976
115 pp. in Spanish

The survey which covered private families of two members and more in the two cities of Panama and Colón, was carried out during the period February, May, August and November of 1972. The purpose of the survey was to collect data to be used in calculating new weights for the Consumer Price Index.

The report, besides presenting information on the survey methodology, organization of field-work, sample selection, methods of collecting data, type of questionnaires used, etc., contains data on total average household expenditure on food and durable goods, also by house-hold income and separately for the cities of Panama and Colón.

PERU

Ing. Curonisy D. and Leonor Laguna, M. Sc.
1)   Encuesta Nacional de Consumo de Alimentos (ENCA)
        Lima, Peru, 15.11.73
        75 leaves in Spanish
2)   Encuesta Nacional de Consumo de Alimentos (ENCA)
        "Analysis del Comportamiento de la Muestra de Viviendas en el Terreno"
        Lima, Peru
        48 leaves in Spanish
3)   ENCA - Reports with different titles and years
        Vol. 1 to 12, 17 to 19 and 22
        Lima, Peru, 1974

The National Food Consumption Survey was organized to obtain information on the consumption behaviour of Peruvian households. It covered the whole national territory during 1971-72.

The first report gives a detailed description of the organization of ENCA 1971-72 and of the methodology of the survey, in particular the sample design, the training of field personnel, the survey execution and results (duration of interview, response, etc.) and the processing of the final data. Some tables at the end of the report complete the information presented in the report.

The second report gives an analysis of the sample distribution in relation to the total population, location, agricultural area, etc., including the level of response.

Other reports give tabulated material on average annual household expenditure for the various items of consumption.

See: Review of Food Consumption Surveys, 1977, Vol. II, FAO, Rome; pp. 258-259 for the tabulated results on food consumption and expenditure.

ST LUCIA

Government of St. Lucia and The Caribbean Food and Nutrition Institute, the Pan-American Health Organization, FAO
The National Food and Nutrition Survey of St. Lucia 1974
The Caribbean Food and Nutrition Institute, Kingston (Jamaica) 1976
(55 pp. and appendices in English)

The survey, which the Government of St. Lucia requested the Caribbean Food and Nutrition Institute to carry out, with the objective of reviewing the food and nutrition status in the country with a view to incorporating a Food and Nutrition Policy into the 5-year National Development Plan, was undertaken in January and February 1974 and covered 1% of the population. The Report of the survey consists of seven chapters. These deal with vital statistics and the agricultural situation in the country, sampling for the survey, residential environments, socio-cultural environments, child feeding, food supply and expenditure patterns. In the appendices to the report some nutritional data are presented together with the 1977 Food Balance Sheet and the Eastern Caribbean Common Market Customs Tariff.

TRINIDAD AND TOBAGO

Government of Trinidad and Tobago and Caribbean Food and Nutrition Institute
Report and Interim Report on National Household Food Consumption Survey in Trinidad and Tobago, 1970
Government Printery, Trinidad, 1972
(74 pp. in English)

The report presents the results of the Household Food Consumption Survey conducted in Trinidad and Tobago during the months of February to May 1970. The survey was a joint project of the Government of Trinidad and Tobago and the Caribbean Food and Nutrition Institute. The survey was conducted over the whole territory to collect adequate information on food consumption needed for the formulation of food and nutrition policies, assessment of malnutrition, future food requirements and distribution of the nutritionally important foods among different segments of the population, establishment of optimal production and distribution objectives and for the preparation of plans for agricultural, public health and economic development.

Part I of the report presents information on the food consumption aspect of the Survey including their correlation with household income, food cost, household sizes and racial differences. Part II of the report deals with the nutritional aspect of food consumption and dietary adequacies.

See: Review of Food Consumption Surveys, 1977, Vol. II, FAO, Rome; pp. 100-101 for a detailed description of the scope and methods of the survey and p. 272-277 for the tabulated results on food consumption.

Central Statistical Office
Household Budgetary Survey 1971/72
Income and Expenditure Patterns
Continuous Sample Survey of Population
Publication No. 22, July 1974
151 pp. in English

The objective of the survey was to collect data for the revision of the existing index of retail prices, for social welfare comparisons, for providing national income statistics, and for use in marketing and econometric analysis and demand studies. The survey was conducted during the period August 1971 to September 1972 in two rounds of 6 months duration. It covered all types of families in Trinidad and Tobago.

Besides outlining some main features of the survey methodology the report provides basic information on the income and expenditure patterns of the household by household income and administrative area. It further provides data on various household characteristics, and on derived statistics including the Gini coefficients and standard errors of survey results.

See: Review of Food Consumption Surveys, 1977, Vol. II, FAO, Rome; p. 102 for a detailed description of the scope and methods of the survey.

Central Statistical Office
Household Budgetary Survey 1975/76 - Report No. 2
Port of Spain - November 1978
143 pp. in English

The survey was conducted by the Central Statistical Office, with several objectives, including the following: study changes in the pattern of household expenditure especially the proportion spent on food; measure household income, expenditure and consumption; revise weights for the index of retail prices; provide estimates of the quantity and value of food purchased and consumed. The survey covered the periods March-September 1975 and October-March 1976, and all types of private households over the whole territory. The report provides some basic information on living conditions of households surveyed as well as on profiles of household expenditures by administrative area, composition of household and selected socio-economic groups of heads of households. It also gives a brief description of the survey methodology used together with highlights of the tables presented.

N E A R   E A S T

Ministry of Finance, Department of Statistics and Research
Household Survey 1971: Republic of Cyprus
Vol.2; Household Expenditure
Ministry of Finance, Dept. of Statistics and Research, Nicosia, Nov.1972
192 pp. in English

The survey was the first full-scale household enquiry to be carried out in Cyprus. As a result, an attempt was made to collect data on most of the socio-demographic and economic aspects of the households. The main objectives were:-

(i)   to acquire detailed information on the standard of living of
        the Cypriot population and thus to supply the basic data
        necessary for policy making in connection with social and
        economic planning;

(ii)   to obtain detailed information on the pattern and structure
        of household expenditures for the revision of the Retail
        Price Index;

(iii)   to supplement the data available for use in compiling official
        estimates of national expenditures;

(iv)   to analyse the variation in family levels of living between
        and within urban and rural areas;

(v)   to provide data on the relationship between the basic character-
        istics of the household, such as size and structure, and the level
        of expenditure and cash disposable income;

(vi)   to furnish information on the level and pattern of expenditures
        of households of differing demographic, economic and social
        characteristics.

The survey covered the entire population living in private households. It excluded the Turkish Community and members and families of the Greek and Turkish contingents stationed on the island, the British Sovereign bases and the members of the diplomatic and other foreign missions.

The survey covered the entire year (1971). This was to ensure that normal expenditure periods and seasonal variations were covered. The year was divided into four survey periods, spaced at three-month intervals. One-quarter of the sampled households was interviewed in each of the four periods.

The report contains parts dealing with survey methodology, objectives, coverage, sample design, concepts and definitions. It presents detailed breakdowns of data on purchases and receipts by variables such as income group, size and structure of households, employment status and occupation of head of household.

See: Review of Food Consumption Surveys, 1977, Vol.II, FAO Rome; pp.39 to 42 for a detailed description of the scope and methods of the survey, and pp. 137 to 139 for the tabulated results on food expenditure.

EGYPT

Central Agency for Public Mobilization and Statistics
National Family Budget Survey 1974-75
Cairo 1976
28 pp. in Arabic

IRAQ

Republic of Iraq, Ministry of Planning, Central Statistical Organisation
Household Budget and Living Conditions Survey 1971-72
First stage: July 1972 - 106 pp. in Arabic and English
Second stage: January 1972 - 111 pp. in Arabic and English
Banghdad (1974).

This enquiry, which was a multi-stage survey on household budget and living conditions, was the first comprehensive survey to cover all regions of Iraq and the different seasons of the year. For this reason, three pilot experimental surveys were undertaken in Baghdad and one in a rural area in May-June 1969 and June 1970. The survey was carried out in three stages, the first stage in July 1971, the second in January 1972 and the third in April 1972. These stages were timed so as to ensure coverage of different seasons of the year.

Reports of the first and second stages (summer and winter) have been published. They consist of an introduction explaining the aim and methodology of the survey, including concepts and techniques used in data processing, and over 100 tables on household and per capita expenditures and quantities of food consumed by various household characteristics. All data are available for urban and rural areas separately.

See: Review of Food Consumption Surveys, 1977, Vol.II, FAO, Rome; pp-63-64 for a detailed description of the scope and methods of the survey, and pp.181-187 for the tabulated results on food consumption and expenditure.

ISRAEL

Central Bureau of Statistics
Family Expenditure Survey 1968/69 - Part IV: Family Income
Special Series No.388
Jerusalem 1972
100 pp., in English and Hebrew

The objective of the survey was to investigate the structure of the budget of urban families and obtain data to be used by research workers on consumption patterns, demand habits and forecasts of consumers' demands, etc.

All urban private families in 76 localities were covered by the survey during the period from September 1968 to August 1969. The families in the sample were divided into 12 parts and each part was investigated in a different month during the survey year.

The report is part of a series of publications in which the final and complete results of the Family Expenditure Survey were presented to the public. It presents a comprehensive set of tables on urban family income. Details of the methodology of the survey and the evaluation of results are also given in the report.

Central Bureau of Statistics
Family Expenditure Survey in the Administered Territories 1973/74
Special Series No.532
CBS, Jerusalem 1976
95 pp. in Hebrew, including a summary in English.

The Family Expenditure Survey 1973/74 of the Administered Territories was commissioned by the Army Administration and carried out by the Central Bureau of Statistics. Its purposes were twofold: to investigate the standard of living of the population in towns and refugee camps, and to update the baskets of the consumer price index. The survey included the families in towns and refugee camps. These constituted a quarter of all families in Judaea and Samaria and about five-sixths of all families in the Gaza Strip. The survey was conducted over the twelve-month period between September 1973 and August 1974.

The report comprises the findings and methods of the survey; it presents averages of consumption expenditure according to various characteristics of the family or family head, e.g. employment status, age, education, family size; it contains data on distribution of families according to the above characteristics as well as by ownership of various household articles and facilities.

Central Bureau of Statistics
Family Expenditure Survey 1975/76
Part A: General Summary
Special Series No.563
CBS, Jerusalem 1978
200 pp. in Hebrew and 45 of English translation. All tables have double headings in Hebrew and English.

The Family Expenditure Survey is one of the largest and most complex surveys carried out by the Central Bureau of Statistics. Its purpose is to investigate the budgets of urban households and to supply information that would serve as a basis for a wide range of uses, such as: demand forecasts, updating the cost of living index basket, studies on the level and composition of incomes and savings, etc. The investigation of households in the survey was conducted over a twelve-month period from June 1975 to May 1976 and the sample was distributed over these months. It covered urban households over the whole territory.

This report is the first of a series of publications in which the Bureau intends to present the findings of the 1975/76 Family Expenditure Survey. The report is designed to convey a general picture of urban households' budgets and composition of their expenditures and incomes; it contains, besides a methodological appendix, a brief description on the survey's findings and tables on households' income and budgets by various household characteristics. Also included are quantities of food consumed. A sample of questionnaires and the diary for daily entries used is included in the report.

Libyan Arab Republic
Technical Planning Body
Census and Statistical Department

1. Report on the First Phase on the Household Sample Survey 1969 (Tripoli Town)
   39 pp. in Arabic and English

2. Report on the Second Phase of the Household Sample Survey 1969 (Tripoli Town)
   Household Expenditure - 42 pp. plus annexes in Arabic and English

3. Report on the First Phase of the Household Sample Survey 1969 (Benghazi Town)
   37 pp. in Arabic and English

4. Report on the Second Phase of the Household Sample Survey 1969 (Benghazi Town)
   42 pp. plus annexes in Arabic and English

Printed at the Census and Statistical Department, 1970.

The main objectives of the survey were to provide basic information on household consumption expenditure and capital transactions, and also information on housing conditions, demographic characteristics of the individuals, occupation, income, and data on internal migration.

The above reports are part of a series of publications containing the results of the Household Sample Survey undertaken by the Census and Statistical Department in 1969.

Reports relating to the first stage, describe the main demographic and economic characteristics of the households and their members. Reports relating to the second phase deal with households' expenditure and capital transactions. All reports consist of a descriptive part on the methodology used, and of a certain number of tables.

See: Review of Food Consumption Surveys, 1977, Vol.II, FAO, Rome; pp.79-81 for a detailed description of the scope and methods of the survey, and p.205 for the tabulated results on food expenditure.

Sudan Nutrition Division

1. Food Consumption Survey in Khartoum - June-August 1971
2. Food Consumption Survey in Soba-West Village - December 1972
3. Food Consumption Survey in Iadd Hussein Village - April 1974
4. Food Intake Survey at Karari Area - December 1972
5. Nasir Extension Food Intake Survey

Around 10 leaflets each in English.

A series of surveys carried out in various parts of the country to elicit a comprehensive picture on the patterns of food intake and other factors affecting them. Some information on survey methods used and the results on data on the nutritive value of food intakes are provided in the report.

Koksal, O.
Haceteppe Universitesi, Ankara
United Nations Children's Fund, Ankara
National Nutrition, health and food consumption survey of Turkey, 1974
Ankara, Haceteppe University, UNICEF, 1977
566 pp. English translation.

This nationwide nutrition survey was carried out in order to assess the nutritional status
of Turkish people and to determine the nutritional problems and their causes. Findings are
presented in six sections and relate to: methodology, demographic characteristics of sample
families, family food consumption, child nutrition, anthropometric measurements, results of
clinical examinations and biochemical tests. Samples of questionnaires used are included in
the report.

See: Review of Food Consumption Survey, 1977, Vol.II, FAO, Rome; pp. 103-104 for a detailed
description of the scope and methods of the survey.

FAR EAST

Bureau of Statistics, Dacca
A Report on the Household Expenditure Survey of Bangladesh, 1973-74:
household consumption statistics by income classification - Vol.I
Ministry of Planning, Bureau of Statistics, Statistics Division, Dacca, Aug. 1978
76 pp. in English.

Since July 1973, the Bangladesh Bureau of Statistics has been conducting sample surveys to collect current information on the expenditure of household consumption items to reflect the changes in the pattern of household consumption expenditure. These surveys are conducted on a quarterly basis in selected urban and rural areas of the country.

This report is based on results of the first series of surveys, covering the period July 1973 to June 1974. The survey covered the whole territory and all private households excluding institutions and those households which depend for their living entirely on charity. The report contains methodological aspects of the survey, such as purpose, reference period, organisation of fieldwork, sample design, data processing and the concepts and definitions used. It presents tables of data on household demographic characteristics, expenditure on food and non-food items by monthly household income classification, and by national, urban and rural breakdowns. Data on quantities of food consumed are also included. Some tables of quarterly data and of annual results, at district and selected city-levels, are also included in the report.

Dacca University, Institute of Nutrition and Food Science
Nutrition Survey of Rural Bangladesh 1975-76
Dacca, University of Dacca, INSF, Dec.1977
237 pp. in English.

The objective of the survey was to study the nutritional status of the rural population in Bangladesh. The survey covered private households in twelve rural localities during the period May 1975 to August 1976.

The study comprised the measurement of dietary and nutritional intake, anthropometric measurements, bio-clinical examinations and the collection of socio-economic data. Seasonality in dietary intake was also studied in some localities selected according to their geographical characteristics and their stage of agricultural development.

The report reviews the methodology of the survey, sample selection, interview methods and the organisation of fieldwork. It also covers aspects of food production and availability in Bangladesh. It gives detailed information on nutritional status and requirements. One chapter of the report deals in particular with the seasonal study.

Samples of questionnaires used are included in the report together with tables containing data on food production and availability, nutritional requirements, dietary intake, intra-family food distribution, anthropometric, clinical and socio-economic data.

See: Review of Food Consumption Surveys, 1977, Vol.II, FAO, Rome; pp.18-19 for a detailed description of the scope and methods of the survey.

Hong Kong Department of Statistics
The Household Expenditure Survey 1973-74 and the Consumer Price Indexes
Hong Kong, Census and Statistics Department 1975   . . .
290 pp. in English.

The main purpose of the Household Expenditure Survey was to furnish information on the
expenditure patterns of certain households in Hong Kong for use in the determination of
a weighting system for a new consumer price index and for making estimates of private consumption expenditure for the estimation of national income and expenditure. The survey
lasted one year, from July 1973 to June 1974 and covered all urban private households
whose monthly consumption expenditure at the time of the survey fell between $400 and
$2,999. Exceptions were single-person households, old persons' households and collective
households living in temporary structures.

The report contains an account of the methodology of the survey, sample design, pilot
survey, response, enumerators' training, interviewing techniques, data processing and cost
and working schedule of the survey. It presents tables giving data on household characteristics and on main items of expenditure by expenditure classes, size of households, number
of earners. A sample of the questionnaires used is also included in the report. There
are special chapters dealing with the Pricing Survey and with the 1973-74 Consumer Price
Index.

See: Review of Food Consumption Surveys, 1977, Vol.II, FAO, Rome; pp.55-56 for a detailed
description of the scope and methods of the survey, and p.151 for the tabulated results on
food expenditure.

National Council of Applied Economics and Research
All India Household Survey of Income, Saving and Consumer Expenditure,
with Special Reference to Middle Class Households
New Delhi 1972
130 pp. in English

The objective of the survey was to estimate and analyse income, savings and expenditure on
selected items of consumption (both durable and non-durable) of the urban and rural household sectors in India for the year 1967-68 (July-June) with special reference to the group
of households having an annual income between Rs.5000 and Rs.15000 (middle class families).

The report presents details of the selection of the urban and rural sample and the main concepts and definitions used in the survey. An analysis of results of household income,
savings and consumer expenditure is also presented. Apart from this, the report presents
66 tables showing data on household income, savings and consumer expenditure by urban and
rural classification, income class and by other variables.

Indonesian Central Bureau of Statistics, Djakarta
Cost of Living Survey 1968-71
Jakarta - Biro Pusat Statistik, 1973 - 10 vols. (over 100 pp. each volume)
in English and Indonesian.

v.2: Bandung, 1968-79; v.3: Jogya Karta, 1968-69; v.4: Surabaya, 1968-69;
v.5: Denpasar, 1968-69; v.6: Medan, 1968-69; v.7: Palembang, 1968-69;
v.8: Ujung Pandang, 1968-69; v.9: Menado, 1970-71; v.10: Banjamarsin 1970-71;
v.11: Pontianak, 1970-71.

The survey aimed at collecting data for calculating new weights for the revision of the consumer price index and at collecting information on social and economic conditions of the
families.

In the first instance the survey was meant to cover the city of Djakarta and a one-year survey period starting April 1968 to March 1969 was envisaged. In the second instance, the survey was extended to another 10 cities and consequently the time coverage prolonged to March 1971. As a result the survey developed into the most comprehensive study of urban family income and expenditure undertaken in Indonesia up to that time. The enquiry was carried out by the Central Bureau of Statistics in all its phases: planning, training of enumerators and supervisors, as well as the processing of survey results.

Each report of the survey presents data relative to one of the eleven cities covered. It consists of two parts: Part 1 gives an introduction explaining the aim of the survey, the sample design adopted, period and methods of data collection, evaluation and processing of results. It also includes a chapter dealing with concepts and definitions. Part 2 gives tables presenting data on economic characteristics of the families, characteristics of the dwelling of the economic family; income receipts and expenditure of the economic family; and a weighting diagram.

See: Review of Food Consumption Surveys, 1977, Vol.II, FAO Rome; pp. 59-60 for a detailed description of the scope and methods of the survey, and p.169-177 for the tabulated results on food expenditure.

Indonesia Central Bureau of Statistics - Djakarta
National Socio-Economic Survey 1969 (4th Round, Oct-Dec.1969)
Provisional Statistics: consumption expenditure: Jawa-Madura, Luar-Jawa
Djakarta 1972 - 64 pp. in Indonesian

National Socio-Economic Survey, Indonesia (5th Round, Jan-Dec.1976)
Consumption Expenditure: Jawa-Madura, Luar-Jawa
Vol.I: Jan.-April 1976: Vol.II: May-Aug.1976: Vol.III: Sept.-Dec.1976
Biro Pusat Statistik, Djakarta 1978 (Indonesian)

The reports consist of an introduction and four or five extensive tables, providing translation of the table headings into English. The tables show data on: population distribution, per capita monthly expenditure by items of consumption, and weekly consumption (quantity) of foods. All data are presented by expenditure classes and for Indonesia as a whole, as well as separately for urban and rural areas and for Jawa-Madura and Luar-Jawa.

See: Review of Food Consumption Surveys, 1977, Vol.II, FAO, Rome; pp.163-168 for the tabulated results on food consumption and expenditure

JAPAN

Bureau of Statistics
Office of the Prime Minister
1974 National Survey of Family Income and Expenditures

Vol.I: Income and Expenditure for Japan; Vol.II: Income and Expenditure for 3 Major Metropolitan Areas; Vol.III: Income and Expenditures by City Groups, City types and Districts; Vol.IV: Income and Expenditure by Prefectures; Vol.V: Expenditure on Commodities; Vol.VI: Expenditure on Commodities by Type of Purchase Place; Vol.VII: Income and Expenditure and Expenditure on Commodities for One-Person Households; Vol.VIII: Savings; Vol.IX: Durable Goods Possessed - Japan - three Metropolitan Areas; Vol.X: Durable Goods Possessed; Vol.XI: Summary Report.
March 1976. In Japanese and summary in English.

This survey has been conducted every five years since 1959. The purpose of the survey is to obtain comprehensive data on income and expenditure of consumer households, quantities of consumer durable goods possessed by them, and on the amounts of savings and liabilities of households all over Japan. The content of each report is as specified in the titles.

A sample of the Family Account Book is included in the publication.

See: Review of Food Consumption Surveys, 1977, Vol.II, FAO, Rome; pp.68-70 for a detailed description of the scope and methods of the survey, and pp. 188-191 for the tabulated results on food expenditure.

Bureau of Statistics
Office of the Prime Minister
Annual Report on the Family Income and Expenditure Survey 1972 through 1976
Published 1973-1977 in Japanese with summary in English.

The Family Income and Expenditure Survey, which started in 1946 and has been carried out annually since then, aims at providing comprehensive data on incomes and expenditures of consumers and other related information. The survey covers all consumer households in Japan except those engaged in agriculture, forestry or fishery, and one-person households. Each annual report consists of three parts: A summary of the income and expenditure of all households and workers' households; statistical tables, and an outline of the survey. The statistical tables show data on receipts and disbursements (110 items) and on household distribution by various characteristics of the household head. Data on quantities of food consumed are also included.

A sample of the Family Account Book is included in the report.

Bureau of Statistics
Office of the Prime Minister
Family Income and Expenditure Survey 1963-75
March 1977
508 pp. in Japanese with summary in English

The survey originates from the Consumer Price Survey initiated in 1946, which took the present title and form in 1962. It is carried out annually and aims at obtaining basic data for throwing light on the status of living of the people and providing statistical data on family income and expenditure by urbanisation and household social and demographic characteristics.

The report contains yearly averages of the results of the Family Income and Expenditure Survey from 1963 to 1975. It also contains statistical tables presenting data on expenditure relating to both workers' households and other households, such as individual proprietors, and of an outline describing the main features of the survey.

KOREA

Republic of Korea
Ministry of Agriculture and Forestry
Report on the Results of Farm Household Economy Survey and Production
Cost Survey of Agricultural Products. 1972. 314 pp. in Korean and English

The survey, which is carried out from January to December each year, covers farm households engaged primarily in farming and cultivating a plot of more than one "tanbo".

The primary objective of this survey is to provide data needed for understanding the rural economy and to measure various aspects of the agricultural structure with a view to improving farm management practices, planning agricultural development and formulating policy measures. The survey would also provide other data which would furnish basic materials for research dealing with agriculture and its contribution to national income. The survey also provides data for estimating production costs of important crops such as rice, barley, wheat. It also furnishes information on farm income, components of income, expenditure, farm assets, liabilities etc., including farm household living expenditures as well as food expenditure.

The report is part of a series of annual reports issued since 1962. It contains the results of the annual survey on the farm household economy and production cost of major agricultural products.

Republic of Korea
Economic Planning Board, Bureau of Statistics
Annual Report on the Family Income and Expenditure Survey
Years: 1968 and 1971 through 1978
in Korean   and English - around 150 pp. each report.

The 'Family Income and Expenditure Survey' is a sample survey carried out annually by the Bureau of Statistics to collect information on the income and expenditure of urban households and changes in their levels of living. The survey covers 35 cities, including Seoul and excludes fishermen's and farmers' households.

Each report consists of an introduction describing the methodology of the survey and of a set of tables on household expenditures by various household demographic and socio-economic characteristics. Sampling errors are given in appendices.

See: Review of Food Consumption Surveys, 1977, Vol.II, FAO, Rome; pp.73-74 for a detailed description of the scope and methods of the survey, and pp.199-202 for the tabulated results on food expenditure.

MALAYSIA

Department of Statistics
Household Expenditure Survey 1973
Summary Statistics
HES Report 1 - Kuala Lumpur 10-01
Malaysia
96 pp. in Malay and English.

The Household Expenditure Survey 1973 is the fourth in a series of studies undertaken in Malaysia on household expenditure. The objective of the survey was to collect comprehensive data on various aspects of household consumption expenditure and on their related economic and demographic characteristics. It covered urban and rural areas in Peninsular Malaysia and six main towns of the states of Sabah and Sarawak. The report presents summary statistics on the results of the survey and also gives an account of the main features of expenditure patterns. It also presents a reconciliation of these data with those of previous surveys and an analysis of broad trends in changes in household expenditure patterns. Household food expenditure data by economic level are also shown, and samples of questionnaires used in the survey are included in the report.

See: Review of Food Consumption Surveys, 1977, Vol.II, FAO, Rome; pp.85-86 for a detailed description of the scope and methods of the survey, and pp.217-221 for the tabulated results on food expenditure.

NEPAL

Nepal Rastra Bank Research Development
Household Budget Survey 1973-1975
Series 1 - Kathmandu, Series 2 - Pokhara, Series 3 - Dhankuta
Kathmandu 1976, 1978.

This household budget survey is an undertaking of the Nepal Rastra Bank. It was carried out during the years 1973-75 and covered 18 selected centres of the country. The survey was conducted for the purpose of obtaining appropriate weighting factors for preparing reliable and comprehensive consumer price index for the country. The results are published in 18 separate series and provide basic information on the social and economic conditions of the people living in the areas covered by the survey.

PAKISTAN

Government of Pakistan
Ministry of Finance, Planning and Development
Statistical Division
Household Income and Expenditure Survey - 1968-69, 1969-70, 1970-71, 1971-72
Karachi 1973. Around 40 pages each annual report, in English

The Household Income and Expenditure Survey was initiated in July 1963 as one of the regular national sample surveys carried out by the Statistical Division. The survey aims at collecting data on household composition; income and its sources; pattern of consumption and non-consumption expenditure; household receipts; disbursements and savings etc. The survey was suspended in July 1972 and it was planned to re-start it on a regular basis in July 1974. Each annual report contains methodological information and several tables presenting data on household composition and living expenditures by income groups. Quantities of food consumed are also shown. The data furnished relate to the urban and rural areas of West Pakistan.

See: Review of Food Consumption Surveys 1977, Vol.II, FAO, Rome; pp.91-92 for a detailed description of the scope and methods of the survey, and pp.235-257 for the tabulated results on food expenditure.

PHILIPPINES

Food and Nutrition Research Institute
National Science Development Board
Food Consumption Surveys. 1 - 1974 Luzon including Greater Manila Area - 27 leaves;
                          2 - 1975 Western Central and Easter Visayas - 34 leaves;
                          3 - 1976 Greater Manila Area - 40 leaves;
                          4 - 1974-75 Sample design and coverage, survey methodology - 25
                              leaves.
All in English.

The reports contain the findings of a series of household food consumption surveys conducted annually by the Food and Nutrition Research Institute during the 1970s. These surveys covered certain geographical areas of the Philippines and were conducted on sample sizes ranging from 680 to 1311 households. The results of dietary consumption levels are compared with recommended nutritional allowances. Only the figures of average consumption are shown in the publications.

SINGAPORE

Department of Statistics
Report on the Household Expenditure Survey 1972/73
Singapore, December 1974
66 pp. in English.

The primary objective of this nationwide survey, the second of its kind conducted in Singapore, was to collect information on the pattern of expenditure of private households and to provide a basis for revising the weighting pattern of the Consumer Price Index. The report consists of a descriptive part relating to the methodology applied, comments on the results of the survey, and of several tables presenting data on household demographic characteristics, occupational status, and on household living expenditures by various household characteristics. A sample of the questionnaires used is included in the report.

Department of Statistics
Report on Survey of Households, April 1977
Department of Statistics, Singapore, March 1978
84 pp. in English

This report contains the results of the first phase of the Household Expenditure Survey covering the whole territory. The survey was conducted in April/May 1977 to collect information on demographic and socio-economic characteristics of the population. Results of phase two of the survey, which was conducted from June 1977 to May 1978 to collect information on patterns of expenditure of private households for the purpose of revising the weighting pattern of the consumer price index, were a subject of another report still to be published.

This report also contains information on the methodology used. A sample of the questionnaire used is also included in the report.

SRI LANKA

Department of Census and Statistics
Socio-Economic Survey of Sri Lanka 1969-70
Rounds 1-4: Statistical Tables
Vol.I: Population, Labour Force and Housing
Vol.II: Household Income Consumption and Expenditure
Dept. of Govt. Printing 1973; 130 and 216 pp. plus appendices (questionnaires)

Special Report on Food and Nutritional Levels
Dept. of Govt. Printing 1972, 35 pp.
Original language: English

The objective of this nationwide survey was to obtain basic data on social and economic conditions of the population for use in the formulation and implementation of social and economic policy. The survey was conducted in consecutive rounds, each of 3 months duration, commencing 1 November 1969.

The report is divided into two volumes. Volume I contains data on demography, educational levels, employment and unemployment, and housing conditions. Volume II contains data on personal income and consumer expenditure as well as a summary of important findings of the survey. Some methodological information is presented in the introduction to the two volumes.

The Special Report on Food and Nutritional Levels contains a methodological note on the socio-economic survey, an evaluation of the findings on food and nutrition levels, and the appendix tables showing the detailed results. Samples of the questionnaires used are included in the report.

Department of Census and Statistics
Ministry of Plan Implementation
Report on the Urban Family Budget Survey 1977
Colombo, November 1978
42 pp. in English, plus appendix (questionnaire)

The survey covered seven of the urban areas of Colombo District, and was conducted during the first quarter of 1977. The objective of the survey was to obtain factual information on social and economic conditions of the urban community, with particular reference to the levels and patterns of income and expenditure of households. The report consists of two parts: Part I contains a summary of the general features of the survey and an evaluation of some of the main findings of the survey. Part II contains a set of tables presenting data on the demographic characteristics of the population, employment and unemployment, housing conditions, and on income levels and expenditure patterns of households. Samples of the questionnaires used are included in the report.

TAIWAN

Bureau of Accounting and Statistics
Taiwan Provincial Government
Report on the Survey of Family Income and Expenditure in Taiwan 1966
June 1968
419 pp. in Chinese and English

The survey was carried out to collect data on household income and expenditure for estimating national income and studying income distribution and levels of living of the population. The report consists of two parts. The first part describes in detail the survey programme, sampling design, analysis of survey data, sampling errors etc. The second part consists of 26 tables showing data on income composition, income and expenditure distribution by various household characteristics.

Department of Budget, Accounting and Statistics
Taiwan Provisional Government
Republic of China
Report on the Survey of Family Income and Expenditure, Taiwan Province
Republic of China 1972, 1973, 1974 and 1975
September 1973; July 1974; June 1975
Original language: Chinese (subtitles in English only for the tables)

Tables' content as for the 1966 survey described above.

THAILAND

National Statistical Office
Office of the Prime Minister
Report Socio-Economic Survey 1969
Publication Series E-Su R - No.3-73
72 pp. in Thai and English

The Socio-Economic Survey, previously called the Household Expenditure Survey, was initiated by the National Statistical Office in 1957 as a national sample survey. It aimed at collecting data on household composition, expenditure on foods and services, income and its source, etc.

The report presents the findings of the third survey conducted from January to September 1969. It consists of a descriptive part covering the survey objectives, sample design, definitions etc., and of the tables showing the distribution of households by various demographic characteristics such as size of household, age of household head, education of household head, etc., and the figures on monthly household expenditure for food, goods and services.

National Statistical Office
Office of the Prime Minister
Report Socio-Economic Survey 1975-76
Northeastern Region: Central Region
Publication Series E-Su R - No.3 and 8-78

The Socio-Economic Survey 1975-76 (see also the report on the 1969 survey described above) was conducted throughout the Kingdom during the period November 1975 - October 1976. Separate reports have been published for the following: Northern Region, Central Region, Northeastern Region, Southern Region and the Greater Bangkok Metropolitan Area. Within the regions, survey results are presented for three types of communities: Municipal Areas, Sanitary Districts and Villages. Households are classified primarily into socio-economic groups based on main source of livelihood, and into decile groups based on level of consumption expenditures. Statistical information obtained in the survey covers income by source, expenditures on goods and services, and the socio-economic characteristics of households and of household members.

VIETNAM

Institut National de la Statistique
Enquête sur les Budgets Familiaux dans les Principaux Centres
Urbaines du Vietnam 1969/70
11 pp. in Vietnamese and French

The survey was carried out to collect data for use in the revision of the consumer price index. It was conducted during 1969-1970 in seven urban centres, namely: Saigon, Cân-Tho, Dalat, Nha-Trang and Da-Nang. Apart from methodological information, data on average food expenditure and other living expenditures have been provided in the report as percentage of total expenditure by family type (semi-rural, workers', middle class, etc.).

EUROPE

Osterreichischen Statistischen Zentralamt

Konsumerhebung 1974
Vol. 1 Ergbenisse fur Osterreich
Vol. 2 Ergbenisse fur Bundeslánder
Vol. 3 SonderausWertungen
Beitrage Zur Osterreichischen Statistik-Heft 420, 441, 514
Wien 1976, 1978
140 to 369 pp. respectively, in German

The food consumption survey is carried out in Austria every ten years. The purpose of the
survey is to study the levels and patterns of household food consumption and expenditure,
revise the weights of the cost of living index, estimate consumption and expenditure aggregates
for national accounts, study the distribution of income and expenditure. It is a nationwide survey carried out in combination with the household budget survey convering urban and
rural areas and the period March 1974 to February 1975. Food consumption data (quantities
and expenditure) also by source of food and expenditure data are available by various household
characteristics.

BELGIUM

Ministère de l'Agriculture
Institut Economique Agricole (I.E.A.)
Panel de Consommateurs
Période Jan-Mars 1975
Panel I.E.A. Nr. 1 et 1/1 March and April 1976
pp. 46 and 277 respectively, in French

Report one is an introduction to the interpretation of the results presented in the second
report which refers to average household food quantities bought, prices paid and expenditure including consumption of own produce; all data are available separately by region,
province, socio-economic conditions and age of household head, income of household, size
of household. The "consumers panel" is a marketing permanent study covering around 3000
households selected proportionately to the total population, which furnish regularly and
in turn for a period of 14 consecutive days the above-mentioned information. It covers
agricultural and horticultural products (i.e. meat, milk and milk products, eggs, fruit,
vegetables and ornamental plants), starting from 1976, fish products will be included in
the survey.

Royaume du Belgique
Ministère des Affaires Economiques
Institut National de Statistique
Enquête sur les Budgets des Ménages 1973-74
Etudes Statistiques Nos. 38, 41, 46, 50 - 1975-1978
pp. 59 to 176 each, in French

The purpose of the survey was to study the levels of living, income and expenditure distribution among families of different socio-economic classes.   The survey was nationwide and
covered households whose head was either a worker, an employee or inactive during the
period March 1973 to March 1974.   The results are published in 4 volumes, the first of
which deals with the survey methodology.   The other reports contain data relating to
income and expenditure including food expenditures by socio-economic group and other household characteristics. Report IV presents the findings of the same surveys in as far as they
relate to independent workers. A sample of the questionnaires used is included.

Danmarks Statistik
Household Budget Survey 1971
Statistiske Undersøgelser No. 34
København, March 1977
330 pp. in Danish with summary in English

The main purpose of the survey was to study the levels and patterns of food consumption and
expenditure. The survey included employee households on a national scale and covered both
urban and rural districts, although entire rural districts without any urban areas were
excluded.   The survey was conducted in 1972/73 in combination with a budget survey based
on a sample of almost thousand households.

The report divided into ten chapters deals with the following: method and definition of the
survey; distribution of the households; real and financial wealth; income earning; transfer
to and from households; use, composition of consumption and savings; consumer credit.
Tables in the appendix refer to these headings.   Samples of questionnaires used are attached
to this report.

Central Statistical Office of Finland
Household Survey 1971
Vol. 1 Household Food Consumption Expenditure
Vol. 2 Household Income and Income distribution
Vol. 3 Consumption of Foodstuffs; Ownership amd mode of
        acquisition of durable goods; Use of leisure
Statistical Surveys Series No. 55
Helsinki 1976 and 1977
369, 112, 196 pp. respectively, in Finnish with translation
of tables' headings in English

The survey aimed at providing information on the structure of consumption of households and data to be used for revising the index of cost of living. It covered the year 1971 and all types of private households in Finland. The food consumption enquiry was effected only on 3512 households of the total 8817 which participated in the household survey. Samples of questionnaires used are included in Vol. 1 which contains data on household consumption expenditure by various household characteristics. Vol. 2 is a detailed study of income distribution and source, by households' characteristics. Vol. 3 presents data on consumption of foods by various household characteristics. An appendix deals in particular with aspects of the valuation of own products and products and benefits in kind.

See: Review of Food Consumption Surveys, 1977, Vol. I, FAO, Rome, pp. 26-27 for the detailed description of the scope and methods of the survey and p. 95 for the tabulated results on food expenditure.

FRANCE

Denis Richard
La Consommation Alimentaire des Français - 1969
Institut National de la Statistique et des Etudes Economiques
Collections de l'I.N.S.E.E. Serie M. No. 11 juillet 1971
224 pp. in French

The objective of the survey is to measure the value, physical quantity and trace the medium trends of the total consumption of each retail product and also to analyse the distribution of consumption among the different categories of households defined by their social and demographic characteristics. The survey which is carried out on a permanent basis by I.N.S.E.E. covers the whole territory.

The report contains a review of the survey methodology, an analysis of the results and tables relating to food consumption (quantity and expenditure) by various household characteristics and food acquisition by place and type of sale.

See: Review of Food Consumption Surveys, 1977, Vol. I, FAO, Rome, pp. 28-29 for the detailed description of the scope and methods of the survey and pp. 96-99 for the tabulated results on food consumption and expenditure.

Marie Amick Mercier
La Consommation Alimentaire en 1976
Les Lieux d'Achats des Produits Alimentaires en 1976
Institut National de la Statistique et des Etudes Economiques
Collections de l'I.N.S.E.E., Serie M. No. 80 et 81 Oct-Nov. 1979
160 and 210 pp. respectively, in French

Since 1965, the I.N.S.EE. has been conducting an on-going enquiry into French food consumption; the enquiry constitutes a direct measure of the food consumption of French households (see the above mentioned report of the 1969 survey "La Consommation Alimentaire des Français").

FRANCE (Cont.)

The volume "La Consommation Alimentaire en 1976" presents the average consumption of food products by individual and by year, by value and quantity, according to the principal socio-demographic criteria employed in the enquiry to characterize households. The second volume presents the breakdown of purchases of household food products according to the different channels of distribution (specialized business, supermarkets, etc.).

FEDERAL REPUBLIC OF GERMANY

Statistisches Bundesamt Wiesbaden
Einkommens-und Verbrauchsstichprobe 1973
Heft 1, 3-7
Ein Kommens-und verbrauchsstichprobe 1978
Heft 1
W. Kollhammer GMBH Stuttgart und Mainz
Between 80 to 300 pp. each report, in German

The main purpose of the sample surveys on income and expenditure is to present the income and consumption pattern of all private households, largely in conformity with the definitions and classifications of national accounts. Moreover, the surveys are to provide to the extent possible a comprehensive insight into the levels of living of households of differing social and economic strata. The survey covers the entire territory of the Federal Republic of Germany and is carried out every 3 to 5 years. Results are published in several volumes, each one containing a descriptive part with a comment on the results, plus statistical tables. One report deals exclusively with the methodology of the survey including also a sample of the questionnaire used; another deals specifically with household food expenditures by various household characteristics such as income, household size, social status of the household head.

See: Review of Food Consumption Surveys, 1977, Vol. I and II, FAO, Rome; Vol. I, pp. 30-32 for a detailed description of the scope and methods of the survey and Vol. II p. 288 for the tabulated results on food expenditure.

GIBRALTAR

Gibraltar Statistics Office
Report on the Gibraltar Family Expenditure Survey 1972/73
City Hall, Gibraltar - December 1973
25 leaves in English

The main purpose of the survey was to collect the necessary data for calculating a new index of Retail Prices. However, the survey also provided valuable information on the standard of living and the distribution òf wealth amongst the prople in Gibraltar.

The survey covered all private households in the territory for the period February 1972 to February 1973. The report describes the methodology adopted and presents data on average household expenditure by main expenditure groups.

GREECE

National Statistical Service of Greece
Household Expenditure Survey 1974
S.8 Levels of Living - Private Income and Expenditure
Athens 1978 - 64 pp. in Greek and English

The Household Expenditure Survey was conducted on a sample basis in the whole country in
the year 1974.   The report contains data mainly on household expenditure classified by
two characteristics of households, namely, size and composition and occupation of household
head; data for all households are available also separately for urban/rural areas.

HUNGARY

Kozponti Statisztikai Hivatal
Haztartasstatisztika 1960 1978
Budapest, over 100 pp. each report, in Hungarian

Annual report on the national household budget and expenditure survey which is carried out
over the whole territory with the purpose of studying the levels and patterns of food consumption and expenditure. The important survey items data are published according to social
stratification. These reports not only provide information concerning the consumption by
social strata but also reveal their income situation and the relation between consumption
and income.

See: Review of Food Consumption Surveys, 1977, Vol. I, FAO, Rome, pp. 41-42 for a detailed
description of the scope and methods of the survey and pp. 101-108 for the tabulated results
on food consumption and expenditure.

IRELAND

Central Statistical Office
Household Budget Survey 1973
Vol. I - Summary Results
The Stationery Office, Dublin 1976 - 115 pp. in English

The objective of the survey was to determine in detail the current patterns of household
expenditure in order to provide revised and more comprehensive weights for the Consumer
Price Index.

The report consists of three parts: Part I is a description of the survey including a list
of basic concepts and definitions, selection of the sample, coverage of survey, field work,
non-response, data processing. Part II gives an evaluation of results covering the sample
limitations, accuracy and reliability, presentation and summary of results. Part III
consists of tables, giving the expenditure pattern including food expenditure, of the average
household for: state, urban areas, rural areas and rural farm households, by various household characteristics.
See: Review of Food Consumption Surveys, 1977, Vol. I, FAO, Rome, pp. 43-44 for a detailed
description of the scope and methods of the survey and pp. 109-114 for the tabulated results
on food expenditure.

Central Statistical Office
Household Budget Survey
Annual Urban Enquiry
1. Results for 1974 (nine months) and 1975 :
    the Stationery Office, Dublin, July 1977, 126 pp. in English
2. Results for 1976: the Stationery Office, Dublin, November 1977, 70 pp. in English
3. Results for 1977 the Stationery Office, Dublin, September 1979, 66 pp. in English

This annual enquiry was initiated in 1974 when field work on the large scale national 1973
Household Budget Survey was terminated. The survey is conducted annually on a continuous
basis by the Central Statistical Office in towns containing 1000 inhabitants or more.
The purpose of the survey is to monitor changes in both the levels and pattern of household
expenditure during the year intervening between the large scale national surveys.   Additional
extensive information is also collected concerning the accommodation of each cooperating
household, and the income and personal characteristics of its members.

Each report consists of three parts: one concerning the description of the survey methodology;
part 2 presents a summary of results in particular on accuracy and reliability and on some
household socio-economic characteristics; part 3 gives the actual results, in particular
household income and expenditure by various household demographic and socio-economic
characteristics.

                                                                ITALY

Istituto Centrale di Statistics (ISTAT)
Indagine Campionaria sui Consumi delle Famiglie Italiane 1969
(Sample survey on Italian household consumption)
Note e Relazioni - Agosto 1971, No. 49
115 pp in Italian

Since 1968 ISTAT has been carrying out a sample survey on household food and non-food items
consumption. The survey is part of a larger survey on labour force and data are collected
quarterly (months of January, April, July, October). The annual averages of this quarterly
survey are then published.

The objective of this nationwide survey is to collect data on the patterns of consumption to
be used specially for the compilation of national economic accounts. The report contains a
description of the survey methodology and some results relating to household expenditure
by geographical area, household size and socio-economic status of household head. A sample
of the questionnaires used is included in the report.

Istituto Centrale di Statistica (ISTAT)
I Consumi delle Famiglie (Household Consumption)
Bollettino Mensile di Statistica
Supplemento No. 1-1976 for 1974 Survey
     "   "   13-1976 " 1975   "
     "   "   8-1977 " 1976   "
     "   " 15-1978 " 1977   "
     "   "   7-1979 " 1978   "
143 pp. each in Italian

The objectives of the survey are to study the levels of household food consumption and expenditure, and the social and economic characteristics and standard of living of Italian families and also to collect data for compiling quarterly and annual average estimates of food expenditure for national accounts. The survey, annual and nationwide, was initiated in 1968 by ISTAT; in 1974 the method of selecting the sample was improved and the results are published annually as a supplement to the Monthly Bulletin of Statistics.

Each report consists of a description of the survey methodology (sample size, methods of data collection, data processing) and of tables reporting data on household expenditure and also on food consumed by various household characteristics.

See: Review of Food Consumption Surveys, 1977, Vol. I, FAO, Rome; pp. 47-49 for a detailed description of the scope and methods of the survey and pp. 115-116 for the tabulated results on food expenditure.

LUXEMBOURG

Service Central de la Statistique et des Etudes Economiques
Cahiers Economique No. 59 - Serie D.
Budgets Familiaux: Enquête 1977
Ministère de l'Economic Nationale - STATEC - December 1978
90 pp. in French

The survey aimed at collecting the necessary data to be used for calculating new weights
for the price index. It was the first nationwide household budget survey to be conducted
in Luxembourg and covered salaried four-person households (workers, employees, managers).

The report contains a description of the survey methodology, an analysis of survey results
and tables relating to average household expenditures and consumption. A sample of the
questionnaires used in included in the report.

NETHERLANDS

B. de Vet
Statistical Department of Labour, Income and Consumption
1974/75 Workers' Budget Enquiry - I. Consumption by Workers' Families
during the period May 1974 - April 1975
Article, 10 pp. (including tables) in English

A summary of the main features of the 1974-75 budget enquiry among workers' families
organized by the Central Statistical Office with the purpose of collecting data useful for
updating the weighting scheme of the index of family consumption.

Data reported in this article refer to the households' main groups of expenditure items
including food cross-classified by the household net income.

NORWAY

Central Bureau of Statistics
Private Households' Consumption 1973
Statistiske Analyser Nr. 24
Oslo 1976
192 pp. in Norwegian with translation into English of
tables' headings and conclusions

The main purpose of the survey was to collect data necessary for the revision of weights
of the consumer price index, as well as to estimate the composition of private consumption
for use in national accounts, and in studying the distribution of income and expenditure.
The survey covered the whole territory and all types of private households.   Previously,
household surveys were undertaken in 1958 and 1967.   Since the year 1973 they have been
conducted annually on the basis of the 1973 survey design.   The report presents information on survey methodology and on the analyses of results in relation to various household
characteristics.   In the appendices the data on consumption expenditure by various household characteristics are shown.

Central Bureau of Statistics
Survey of Consumer Expenditure 1974-1976
Norges Offisielle Statistikk B9
Oslo 1979
228 pp. in Norwegian with English summary

The principal aim of these nation wide annual surveys was to give a detailed description
of the consumption pattern of private households in order to update the weights used in
calculating the consumer price index. Besides this the purpose of the survey was to study
the consumption of various groups of households.

The report presents information on survey methodology, survey design, reliability of results,
correction for non-response and analysis of some results. The data reported are those
registered in the surveys of consumer expenditure undertaken in 1974, 1975 and 1976. Expense
per household is an average of the households' expenses for the period 1974-1976 calculated
at 1976 prices. For conversion of the value figures in 1974 and 1975 the consumer price
index was used. The quantity consumption of food is an average of the years 1975-1976.
A sample of the questionnaires used is attached to this report.

POLAND

Glowny Urzad Statystyczny
Budzety gaspodarstu domowch W 1976 r.
(Household Budget Survey)
Warszawa, 1977, 190 pp. in Polish

Since 1973, the Household Budget Surveys in Poland were greatly extended to cover all the
basic groups of the population. The survey is conducted annually and the data are
collected throughout the entire calendar year. Besides, data on general household
expenditures, the information presented in the report covers expenditure on food products
and beverages and on quantities of food purchased or otherwise obtained by household
characteristics such as income, socio-economic groups, and other demographic characteristics.
In the introduction the methodology of the survey is described.

SPAIN

Ministerio de Planificacion del Desarollo
Instituto Nacional de Estadística
Encuesta de Presupuestos Familiares (Julio 1973-Junio 1974)
Metodología y Resultados
Madrid - Mayo 1975
179 pp. plus tables, in Spanish

The Family Budget survey covered the whole national territory and all types of private households. It was undertaken by the National Statistical Institute and aimed at studying the
levels and patterns of food consumption and expenditure besides collecting data to be used
for updating the cost of living index. Within the framework of the household budget and
expenditure survey a food consumption enquiry was carried out.

SPAIN (Cont.)

The report includes information on the survey methodology: concepts, time reference, sample design, field work, data processing, non-response, data reliability and sampling errors. The data reported relate to income, savings, distribution of the sample and household expenditure by households of various characteristics, such as those relating to degree of urbanization, income, household size, etc.

See: Review of Food Consumption Surveys, 1977, Vol. I, FAO, Rome, pp. 59-62 for a detailed description of the scope and methods of the survey and p. 125 for the tabulated results on food expenditure.

SWEDEN

National Central Bureau of Statistics
The Family Expenditure Survey 1969
Preliminary Results
Statistical Report P 1971: 9
Stockholm - April 1971
196 pp., plus tables, in Swedish and introductory notes also in English

The Family Expenditure Survey 1969, was undertaken by the Survey Research Institute of the National Central Bureau of Statistics.   The purpose of the survey was mainly to obtain information on the size of household consumption of different goods and services and the distribution of consumption on household groups.   It covered all types of private households in the country.

The report contains a description of the survey methodology used and results of the survey giving data on consumption by various household characteristics including income.   Also included are data on the structure of the sample.   A sample of the questionnaires used is included in the report.

See: Review of Food Consumption Surveys, 1977, Vol. I, FAO, Rome, pp. 63-64, for a detailed description of the scope and methods of the survey and p. 126 for the tabulated results on food expenditure.

Ministry of Agriculture, Fisheries and Food
Household Food Consumption and Expenditure: 1977
Annual Report of the National Food Survey Committee
London, H.M.S.O. 1978
199 pp. English (Annual Reports available since 1950)

This annual survey covers all private households in Great Britain (i.E. England, Scotland
and Wales, excl. Northern Ireland). The survey serves several objectives, e.g. study of
levels and patterns of average household food consumption and expenditure, s-udy of
nutritional adequacy of average diets of groups of households in relation to requirements;
revision of weights for the calculation of the general index of retail prices; household
demand analysis, etc. Annual reports consist of an analysis of survey results and of
tables relating to household food consumption, expenditure and prices by various household
characteristics including income. The report contains data on the average nutritional
value of food consumed. In the appendices to the report a description of the survey
methodology is included.

See: Review of Food Consumption Surveys, 1977, Vol. I, FAO, Rome, pp. 67-69 for a detailed
description of the scope and methods of the survey and pp. 133-140 for the tabulated results
on food consumption and expenditure (years 1970-1973).

Department of Employment
Family Expenditure Survey 1978
Government Statistical Service, H.M.S.O. - London 1979
171 pp. in English
Other years reports, since 1957/59, are available.

The Family Expenditure Survey (FES) provides a wealth of information about private households and how they spend their money. The survey is based on a representative sample of
private households in the United Kingdom. It has been in operation on a continuous basis
since 1959. The main objective of the survey is to provide information on spending
patterns of households for the calculation of the Retail Price Index. The survey has now
developed into a multi-purpose survey providing a wide range of socio-economic data on
households. The report consists of two introductory narrative sections describing the
survey and the charts and tables contained in the report, and of charts and tables on household characteristics, household expenditure and income. In the various appendices to the
report, data on standard errors, comparisons of survey results with those obtained from the
surveys and on other related analysis are presented.

Socialist Federal Republic of Yugoslavia
Federal Institute of Statistics
Survey on Family Budgets of Workers' households in:
1972: Statistical Bulletin No. 799, Beograd 1973
1973: Statistical Bulletin No. 853,   "   1974
1975: Statistical Bulletin No. 965,   "   1976
1976: Statistical Bulletin No.1028,   " ·   1977
1977: Statistical Bulletin No.1085,   "   1978

Over 40 pp. each in Serbo-Croatian

The survey is undertaken regularly by the Federal Institute of Statistics. It collects
information on total income and expenditure on goods and services and covers three and four-
member households of workers engaged in the public and private sectors of the economy in a
large number of towns found in the country. Results of this survey are published, as
reflected above, in the various issues of the Statistical Bulletin. The data reported
comprise monthly expenditure on food, goods and services by major food groups and by income
group of the population.

See: Review of Food Consumption Surveys, 1977, Vol. I, FAO, Rome, pp. 77-78 for a detailed
description of the scope and methods of the survey and pp. 158-161 for the tabulated results
on food expenditure (years 1969 and 1970).

Socialist Federal Republic of Yugoslavia
Federal Institute of Statistics
Survey on Rural Households
1973: Statistical Bulletin No. 870, Beograd 1974
1974: Statistical Bulletin No. 928,   "   1975
1975: Statistical Bulletin No. 976,   "   1976
1976: Statistical Bulletin No.1952,   "   1977
1977: Statistical Bulletin No.1096,   "   1978
Over 40 pp. each in Serbo-Croatian - Summary in English for Bulletin No. 870.

The Federal Institute of Statistics in collaboration with the statistical institutes of the
socialist republics and provinces, carries out the survey on rural households, formerly
the survey on individual agricultural holdings, since 1952. The survey collects data on
funds, production, consumption, budget and stocks of households on individual agricultural
holdings.

Results are regularly published in the various statistical bulletins as shown above and
refer to household income, monetary receipts and expenditures, household distribution by
socio-economic characteristics, consumption of food.

N O R T H   A M E R I C A

Statistics Canada
Family Food Expenditure in Canada 1969
Vol.I and II
Information Canada - Ottawa, May 1972
208 and 127 pp. in English and French

The reports present results obtained from a survey of family food expenditure in Canada conducted throughout 1969. It was the first food survey of national scope since 1949 and was designed to provide information covering both the urban and rural population. Vol.I contains data relating to detailed average food expenditures and quantities for families and unattached individuals living in Canada, within urbanization size groups and regions. Vol.II presents data showing the relationships between food expenditures and various family attributes, such as family income and family composition. Methodological information on sample design and selection, survey methods and procedures, survey response, definitions, can be found in the introduction. A facsimile of the questionnaire used is included in the report.

See: Review of Food Consumption Surveys, 1977, Vol.I, FAO, Rome, pp.18-20 for a detailed description of the scope and methods of the survey and pp.87-92 for the tabulated results on food expenditure.

Statistics Canada
Family Expenditure in Canada 1969
Vol.I - All Canada: Urban and Rural
Vol.II - Regions
Information Canada - Ottawa, January 1973
199 and 261 pp. in English

The 1969 survey is the first family expenditure survey of national scope since 1948 and was designed to provide information on families and unattached individuals living in private households in all areas of Canada, both urban and rural. The report presents tabulations relating to calendar year 1969 but collected during the first three months of 1970. These data cover family expenditure classified by selected characteristics such as province, urbanization, size class of family, family type, income, tenure, age of head, occupation of head, education of head, country of origin and immigrant arrival year.

An introduction to Vol.I covers the methodology of the survey, specifically sample design and selection, survey methods and the reliability of survey results, eligibility criteria and level of response, presentation of results and definitions used. A facsimile of the questionnaire used is included in the report.

Statistics Canada
Urban Family Food Expenditure 1974
June 1977, 253 pp. in English and French

This survey was the first to cover families' food expenditure in detail since 1969. It covered urban families in 14 major cities of Canada and was conducted throughout the year 1974.

The survey comprised two samples drawn from the Labour Force area sample. One of these samples was designed for the main function of the survey, which was to collect data from families and unattached individuals representing all private households in the 14 cities. For the other sample, families and unattached individuals were screened on the basis of family size and income in a first phase interview, and units specially selected were asked to provide information in the second phase identical to that collected in the main part of the survey. This special part of the survey was designed to collect information on families and unattached individuals at the lower end of the income distribution to selectively increase the number of such units providing complete data in the overall survey.

The report, after describing the methodology of the survey, presents a series of tables showing data on average weekly food expenditure and quantity consumed per family by various household demographic or economic characteristics. A sample of the questionnaire used is included.

Statistics Canada
Urban Family Expenditure 1974
Ottawa, July 1977 – 177 pp. plus annexes in English and French

This report presents the results of the eleventh Survey of Urban Family Expenditure, carried out by Statistics Canada since 1953, when a series of small-scale continuing surveys was initiated. The survey was carried out in January, February and March 1975 and refers to the calendar year 1974. The sample was concentrated on 14 major urban centres. The report contains highlights of the survey methodology and a series of tables reporting family living expenditures by various household demographic and economic characteristics. Samples of questionnaires used are included.

Statistics Canada
Urban Family Food Expenditure 1976
Ottawa, April 1978
240 pp. plus annexes in English and French

This survey was conducted throughout the calendar year 1976, and covered eight major cities. As in previous surveys (see Urban Family Food Expenditure 1969 and 1974) the eight-city sample was drawn from the Labour Force Area Sample, and covered families and unattached individuals.

Besides highlighting the survey methodology and major findings, the report contains tables presenting data on families' consumption and expenditure on foods by various household economic and demographic characteristics.

Samples of questionnaires used are included.

GREENLAND

Danmarks Statistik
Forbrus, opsparing og ind Komster i lø nmodtagerhusstande i Grønland 1968-69
(Household income and expenditure survey)
Statistiske Undersøgelser No.28
København, 1971, 58 pp. in Danish

The report contains an analysis on the findings of the survey and various tables on household expenditures, including food expenditures also by income group.

United States Department of Labor
Bureau of Labor Statistics
Consumer Expenditure Survey: Integrated Diary and Interview Survey Data, 1972-73
Bulletin No.1992 - 1978
136 pp. in English

The primary purpose of the survey was to gather data necessary to revise the market basket and item sample for the Consumer Price Index. The 1972-73 Consumer Expenditure Survey consisted of two separate components, each with its own questionnaire and independent sample: (1) A quarterly interview panel survey in which each consumer unit in the sample was visited by an interviewer every three months over a 15-month period and (2) a diary or record-keeping survey completed by respondents for two consecutive one-week periods. The survey was nationwide. This report is the firt bulletin from the 1972-73 Survey to integrate data from both the diary and interview components in order to present a complete account of consumer spending and income classified by important family characteristics including income. The methodology of integration is also described in the Bulletin.

UNITED STATES

United States Department of Agriculture
Statistical Reporting Service
Farm-Operator Family Living Expenditures for 1973
Washington D.C. May 1975
57 pp. in English

Major purposes of this survey were: to provide weights reflecting farm-operator family living expenditure patterns for a recent year to use in calculating the Index of Prices Paid by Farmers for Commodities and Services, including Interest, Taxes and Farm Wage Rates; to improve benchmark data for estimating farm family living expenses and budgets; to provide estimates of many farm family living expenditures not available from other sources.

The survey was nationwide and covered 2621 farm-operator families.

The report presents data relating to family living expenditures by household economic class as well as describing survey methodology.

O C E A N I A

Australian Bureau of Statistics
Household Expenditure Survey 1974-75
Bulletins: No.1 - An outline of concepts, methodology and procedures
             No.2 - Preliminary results
             No.3 - Standard errors
             No.4 - Expenditure classified by income of households
             No.5 - Quarterly expenditure patterns
             No.6 - Expenditure classified by household composition
             No.7 - Income distribution
             No.8 - Expenditure classified by selected household characteristics
Canberra, Australia - ABS, 1977-78 (in English)

This survey, which was undertaken by the Australian Bureau of Statistics, was designed to find out how the expenditure pattern of private households varies according to income level and other characteristics such as size and composition of household, age and occupational status of the household head. This survey was confined to capital cities. All households living in private dwellings were covered in the survey which lasted twelve months, from July 1974 to June 1975. A second survey has been conducted during the years 1975-76 and covers non-metropolitan areas.
Each bulletin consists of about 80 pages, giving information as specified in the titles. Methodological information relates to objectives, scope, coverage, sample design, response and method of collection of data. A facsimile of questionnaires used is also included in the Appendix.

Bureau of Statistics
Fiji Household Income and Expenditure Survey 1973
Govt. Printer, Suva - September 1974
33 pp. in English

The purpose of the survey was mainly to update the weights for the consumer price index, and to assess changes in the patterns of consumption. The survey lasted six weeks and covered the principal urban centres of Fiji. The report of the survey gives a description of the survey methodology and presents tables on household expenditure, including food, income and demographic characteristics, supplemented by short comments. A facsimile of the schedule used to collect data on household income and demographic characteristics is included in the report.

Bureau of Statistics
A Report on the Urban Household Income and Expenditure Survey in Fiji 1972
Bureau of Statistics, Suva - July 1972
61 leaves (English)

The survey was conducted with the purpose of assessing the changes in the spending habits of households which had taken place since the last (1968) survey was conducted. Besides this, new weights were to be calculated from survey results for the consumer price index. The survey covered the seven major urban areas of Fiji, i.e., Suva, Nausori, Nadi, Labasa, Sigatoka, Ba, Lautoka and lasted six weeks.

The report describes the methodology adopted and presents the analyses of data on income and expenditure, including food expenditure, with particular reference to definition, composition and distribution. Tables in the Appendix refer to weights for a new consumer price index and to the classification of expenditure by economic activity. A sample of the questionnaire used is included in the report.

See: Review of Food Consumption Surveys, 1977, Vol.I, FAO, Rome; pp. 23-25 for a detailed description of the scope and methods of the survey and p.94 for the tabulated results on food expenditure.

NEW CALEDONIA

Institut National de la Statistique et des Etudes Economiques
Les Budgets Familiaux en Nouvelle Caledonie 1969
1ère partie: Resultats d'enquête
2ème partie: Tableaux Statistiques
INSEE, Paris - 236 and 251 pp. respectively, in French

The survey on income, consumption and expenditure was meant to study the levels of living of the people living in New Caledonia without ethnic distinction. It was carried out from June 1968 to July 1969 both in urban and rural areas of the territory. Part one of the report consists of a description of the survey methodology and of an analysis of the results relating to household income, expenditure and budgets' balance. Part two consists of statistical tables on the composition of the sample and on household income and expenditure, including food expenditure, by various household characteristics.

NEW ZEALAND

Department of Statistics
Household Sample Survey 1 July 1973 - 30 June 1974
Department of Statistics, Wellington, August 1975
26 pp. in English

The objective of the survey was to provide details of expenditure patterns of private households in New Zealand. The survey was carried out during the period July 1973 to June 1974 and covered the whole territory. Some details on the data collection procedures, sample design, comparison with previous surveys' results, and on definitions can be found in the report together with tables presenting data on household income and expenditure, including food expenditure, by household income, size, composition, occupation, household head's age and sex.

Department of Statistics
Household Survey Report 1976/77
Department of Statistics Publication
Wellington, December 1977
60 pp. in English

This publication, similar to the one relating to the 1973-74 Survey, contains some methodological information and tables with data on household income and expenditure by household income, size, composition, occupation, household head's age and sex. It contains information not only for the 1976/77 survey but also for the previous two years which for various reasons could not be published earlier. Since 1973/74, the survey has been undertaken every year on a smaller sample. The objective of this annual survey is to provide details of expenditure patterns of private households in New Zealand.

PAPUA AND NEW GUINEA

Shadlow, J.J.
Bureau of Statistics
Papua New Guinea Household Expenditure Survey 1975/76
Preliminary Bulletins: No.1 – Preliminary results for Port Moresby
                       No.2 – Preliminary results for Lae
                       No.3 – Preliminary results for Kieta, Arawa, Panguna
                       No.4 – Preliminary results for Rabaul
                       No.5 – Preliminary results for Goroka
Port Moresby, Bureau of Statistics, 1977
Each Bulletin of around 50 pp. each in English

The survey was conducted in six major urban centres, specifically: Port Moresby, Lae, Goroka, Rabaul, Madang and Kieta/Arawa/Panguna, from September 1975 to February 1976 and covered only private dwellings occupied by Papua New Guineans. The purpose of the survey was to review the composition of the basket of goods and services for use in calculating the consumer price index and obtain information on income distribution, housing and other socio-economic conditions.

Each bulletin contains some information on methodology and results relating to: comparison of income and expenditure, household expenditure on selected items, cash income, household demographic characteristics. These results are based on advanced hand tabulations.

See: Review of Food Consumption Surveys, 1977, Vol.I, FAO, Rome; pp.93-94 for a detailed description of the scope and methods of the survey.

WESTERN SAMOA

Department of Statistics
The Report on the Survey of Household Living Conditions in Western Samoa 1971-72
Ama, Western Samoa, September 1972
118 pp. in English

The survey covered a variety of subjects, mainly information on size and composition of households, housing conditions, source of income and expenditure. It was the first survey of this kind to be conducted in the country. It was conducted over the whole territory during the period August 1971 to January 1972. The report presents information on survey methodology and tables on household demographic characteristics, household income and patterns of food and non-food expenditures. A facsimile of the questionnaire used is also included in the report.

PART II

TABULAR SUMMARY
OF
SCOPE, METHODS AND RESULTS OF SURVEYS

EXPLANATORY NOTES AND LEGEND ON THE SYNOPTIC TABLES

REGIONS: AFRICA, LATIN AMERICA, NEAR EAST, FAR EAST, NORTH AMERICA, EUROPE AND OCEANIA

Columns	Explanatory Notes and Legends
(1) Country and Title of Survey	Name of the country. These are grouped by the above regions and listed in alphabetical order. The exact title of the survey as specified in national reports or publications.
(2) Year of the Survey	The year(s) in which the survey was actually conducted.
(3) Type of Survey	Various types of surveys are the source of information on food acquired or consumed. Distinction is made between:

FC: Food Consumption Surveys
FB: Family Budget or Household Consumption and Expenditure Surveys
N: Nutrition Surveys
O: Other Surveys (specified)

(4) Geographical coverage   Indicates the geographical area covered as specified in survey reports according to the following:

NW: Nationwide
R: Rural
U: Urban

In addition, if limited to one or more areas or towns, the names of these have been indicated.

(5) Population coverage   Indicates the type of households or individuals covered or excluded from the survey.

(6) Sample size   Indicates the number of households or individuals actually covered or planned to be covered in the survey sample, whichever is available. If both are available, the number refers to the final sample used.

(7) Duration of the Survey   Time period the survey lasted in the field.

(8) Methods of Enumeration   The methods by which the data were collected from respondents:

I: Interview
RK: Record Keeping
DM: Direct Measurement.

(9) Reporting Period   The time period for which records of food acquired or consumed were taken.

Results

(10) Type   Whether estimates of food acquired or consumed are expressed in terms of:

E: Expenditure
Q: Quantities
N: Nutrients

Nc = calories
Np = proteins
Nf = fats
Nv = vitamins
Nm = minerals
Others (specified)

(11) Unit   The unit by which the average results have been presented

                 H: Household
                 C: Per capita units
               CU: Consumption units
               O: Others (specified)

(12) Classification Indicates whether results given under column (12), i.e. E, Q, N,
     and cross-   are tabulated by classifications or cross-classifications of
     classifications variables given below:

                 I: Income groups
                 E: Expenditure groups
                 G: Geographical/Urbanisation group
               SE: Socio-Economic group
               HDC: Any household demographical characteristics such as household
                        size, composition, education of head of household etc.
                 S: Season.

(13) Other results The column presents other relevant results available, e.g. anthropometric measurement, food habits and restrictions, meal preparation,
etc. Also other calculations or studies made from survey results such
as comparisons with scales of nutritional requirements and allowances,
demand analysis, time series analysis, income elasticities, comparison
with other survey results, sampling errors, evaluation of survey
results etc.

Explanation of Signs used in the Tables

...   information not available
X   information available
---   none or nil.

	Country and Title of Survey (1)	Year of Survey (2)	Type of Survey (3)	Geographical coverage (4)	Social coverage (5)	Sample size (6)	Duration of Survey (7)	Method of Enumeration (8)	Reporting period (9)	Results Type (10)	Results Unit (11)	Nº of food groups/ items covered (12)	Classi-fication & cross classi-fication (13)	Other results (14)
AFRICA														
Algeria	Rapport sur la Situation Alimentaire en Algerie	1976/77	FC	Rural areas, Northern part of the country	Agricultur-al workers, private sec-tor of agri-culture	2,500	One year	DM	7 days	Q Nc Np	C C C	50 Total food Total food	SE Season Season	
Botswana	Household Expenditure Survey	1968-70	FB	Population centres of: Serowe Malepole Maun Urban areas: Francistown Lobatse Gaborone	Private households	2,024	One year	...	One month	E	H	29	I	
Burundi														
	Enquête Sta-tistique Ali-mentaire et Budgetaire	1970-71	FB/FC	Rural area Regions of: Ngozi Muyinga	Rural households	515 545	One year	I	28 and 7 days three times in year for FB and FC sur-vey	Nc Np Nf Nv Nm E	C	15	G 1/ O 1/	
	Enquête au-près des Men-ages de Bujumbura	1978-79	FB	Bujumbura	Private households	1,603	One year	I	21 days	E		Total food	G 1/ O 1/	Final results not yet available

1/ Cash value of consumption

(1) Country and Title of Survey	(2) Year of Survey	(3) Type of Survey	(4) Geographical coverage	(5) Social coverage	(6) Sample size	(7) Duration of Survey	(8) Method of Enumeration	(9) Reporting period	Results (10) Type	Results (11) Unit	(12) Nº of food groups/items covered	(13) Classification & cross classification	(14) Other results

Chad

| Enquête Budget Consommation à N'Dhamena | 1970-71 | FB | Fort-Lamy | Private households | 60 | One year | I | One week for consumption one month for expenditure 1/ | E | H | 96 | I S I x S | |

Central Africa

| Enquête Budget et Consommation des Menages | 1975/76 | FC FB N | Nationwide | Private households | 1530 | One year | ... | ... | E Q Nc | H | 14 | G SE HDC G x SE G x HDC | Prices Type of meals consumed |

Kenya

| Urban Food Purchasing Survey | 1977 | Marketing Survey | Nairobi Mombasa Nakuru Kisumu | Private households with income limits | ... | One year | I | One month | E | H | 10-17 | I G HDC SE | |

Lesotho

Extract from the Report on the Rural Household Consumption & Expenditure Survey	1967-69	FB	Rural	Farming households	1797	One year	I	Week	E	H	9	G x I	
Urban Household Budget Survey Report	1922/73	FB	Urban All lowlands towns	Private households	412 per month	One year	RK	One month	E	H	77 16	I I x G	Food habits Fertility
Report of the 1973 Lesotho Pilot Survey on Population & Food Consumption	1973	FC N	16 villages in eight districts	Private households	150	One month	I DM	One week	Nc Np	E	Total food	I	

(1) Country and Title of Survey	(2) Year of Survey	(3) Type of Survey	(4) Geographical coverage	(5) Social coverage	(6) Sample size	(7) Duration of Survey	(8) Method of Enumeration	(9) Reporting period	Results (10) Type	(11) Unit	(12) No of food groups/items covered	(13) Classification/ & cross classification	(14) Other results
Madagascar													
Enquête sur les Budgets des Menages Malgaches a Tananarive ville	1968–69	FB	Urban city of Tananarive	Malagasyan households	480	One year	I	30 days	E	H	11	SE	
Enquête sur les Budgets des Menages en milieu rural	1968–69	FB N	Rural (Antanifotsy; Moroansetra; Morondava; Vohipeno)	Rural households	480	One year	I	30 days	E	H	11	G; I x G; E x G	
Enquête sur les Dêpenses des Menages Etrangères a Tananarive ville	1969	FB	Urban city of Tananarive	Foreigners' households	113	4 May–15 June	RK I	14 days	E E	H H	34 Total food	SE E	
Malawi													
Household Income and Expenditure Survey	1968	FB	Six areas: Blantyre Zomba Lilongwe Mzuru Small urban areas Agricultural estates	Private households	3890	One year	I	7 days (recall)	E	H	94	I x G	
Morocco													
La Consommation et les Dêpenses des Menages au Maroc	1970–71	FB FC	Nationwide	Private households	6546	One year	I	One week	Q; Nc; Np Nf; Nv Nm	C C	55 14	SE x G E; E x G SE SE x G G; E; G x E	

(1) Country and Title of Survey	(2) Year of Survey	(3) Type of Survey	(4) Geographical coverage	(5) Social coverage	(6) Sample size	(7) Duration of Survey	(8) Method of Enumeration	(9) Reporting period	Results (10) Type	Results (11) Unit	(12) Nº of food groups/items covered	(13) Classification & cross classification	(14) Other results
Réunion													
Enquête sur les Revenus et Dépenses des Ménages de la Réunion	1976–77	FB	Nationwide	Private households	1342	One year	I RK	7 days	–	–	–	–	
Rwanda													
Une Enquête de Consommation Alimentaire au République Rwandaise	1966–72	FC N	Nationwide	Private households	...	5-6 years	I	7 days	Q; Nc Np; Nf	C	33	G	
Senegal													
Budget Consommation	1975	FB FC	Dakar	African households	544	One month	U	One month	E E	H H;CU	Total food 65	E; HDC; O E	
Sierra Leone													
Household Survey	1966–70	FB	Nationwide	Private households	3000	1966–70 in various phases	I	30 days	E Q	H C; H	15 6	I; G I x G HDC G x I	Seasonal variation in food consumption

1/ Of which 203 were canvassed for the consumption study

Country and Title of Survey	Year of Survey	Type of Survey	Geographical coverage	Social coverage	Sample size	Duration of Survey	Method of Enumeration	Reporting period	Results Type	Results Unit	Nº of food groups/items covered	Classification & cross classification	Other results
(1)	(2)	(3)	(4)	(5)	(6)	(7)	(8)	(9)	(10)	(11)	(12)	(13)	(14)
Somalia Mogadishu Family Budget Survey	1977	FB	Mogadishu	Private households	768	March'77 Dec.'77	I	One week	E E	H C	80 7	E E	Retail prices. Housing conditions.
South Africa Survey of Household Expenditure	1975	FB	13 Urban areas	White population	4677	One year	–	One month	E	H	132	G x O	
Tanzania Household Budget Survey	1969	FB	Nationwide	Private households	3000	One year	I [1]	2 months urban; 1 year rural	E Q	H H	20 143	E x G G x HDC G x SE E x G G	
Tunisia Enquête nationale sur les Budgets et la Consommation des Menages	1975	FB FC N	Nationwide	Private households	4962[2]	One year	I DM	One week	E Q Q Nc;Np;Nf Nm:Nv Nc;Np;Nf	C C C C C Total food	14 14 64 11	G; HDC SE; E G G G E	Nutrition requirements. Coefficient of elasticity of expenditure and quantity

[1] One interview/month/year in rural area; one interview/tendays/two months in urban area (Dar-es-Salaam)

[2] Of which 50% only took part in the food consumption survey.

(1) Country and Title of Survey	(2) Year of Survey	(3) Type of Survey	(4) Geographical coverage	(5) Social coverage	(6) Sample size	(7) Duration of Survey	(8) Method of Enumeration	(9) Reporting period	Results		(12) Nº of food groups/ items covered	(13) Classification & cross classification	(14) Other results
									(10) Type	(11) Unit			
Zaire													
Budgets Ménagers, Nutrition et Mode de Vie à Kinshasa	1969	FB	Kinshasa	African households	1471	One year	I	One month	E; Nc;Np Nf;Nv Nm	H; CU	97 Total food	I	Elasticity coefficients. Nutritional analysis.
Enquête des Budgets Familiaux en Milieu Africain	1971	FB	Bukavu	Private households	295	One month	I	30 days	E; Q;Nc Np;Nf Nv;Nm	H; H,C	100; 14	–; Economic level	Retail prices. Housing conditions. Elasticity coefficients
Food and Nutrition Survey in the Mbanza-Ngungu Region	1975	FC N	Mbanza-Ngungu Region, both urban and rural	Private households	186	23 days	I DM	20 days budget, 5 days consumption	E; Q; N	H; C; C	9; 133 Total food	E x G; 1/x G; 0—1/x G; E x G SE	Malnutrition
Zimbabwe													
Report on the Urban African Budget Survey in Bulawayo	1968	FB	Bulawayo	Private households	517	35 days	I	One month	E	H	51	I	New weights for consumer price index
Report on the Urban African Budget Survey in Salisbury	1969	FB	Salisbury	Private households	568	26 Sept- 5 Dec.	I	One month	E; Q	H; CU	51; 25	I; I	New weights for consumer price index
Report on the European Family Budget Survey in Salisbury	1969/ 71	FB	Salisbury	Private households	797	Continuous survey covering 24 h/holds per month	RK I	One month	E	H	51	I	New weights for consumer price index

1/ Number of budget units per household.

(1) Country and Title of Survey	(2) Year of Survey	(3) Type of Survey	(4) Geographical coverage	(5) Social coverage	(6) Sample size	(7) Duration of Survey	(8) Method of Enumeration	(9) Reporting period	(10) Results Type	(11) Results Unit	(12) Nº of food groups/items covered	(13) Classification & cross classification	(14) Other results
Zimbawe (contd.)													
Report on the Urban African Budget Survey in Midlands	1970	FB	Gwelo Que Que Gatoona	Private households	570	26 Sept-31 Oct. 1 Nov.- 5 Dec.	I	One month	E Q	H CU	51 25	I I	New weights for consumer price index.
Report on the Urban African Budget Survey in Umtali	1971	FB	Umtali	Private households	597	"	I	One month	E Q	H CU	51 14	I I	New weights for consumer price index
European Expenditure Survey	1975/ 76	FB	Salisbury Bulawayo Umtali Gwelo	Private households	206 252 133 109	Jan.'75- Dec.'76. Continuous survey covering 24 h/holds per month	RK I	One month	E	H	51	I	New weights for consumer price index.

LATIN AMERICA AND CARIBBEAN ISLANDS

Country and Title of Survey	Year of Survey	Type of Survey	Geographical coverage	Social coverage	Sample size	Duration of Survey	Method of Enumeration	Reporting period	Results Type	Results Unit	Nº of food groups/items covered	Classification & cross classification	Other results
(1)	(2)	(3)	(4)	(5)	(6)	(7)	(8)	(9)	(10)	(11)	(12)	(13)	(14)
Bahamas Household Budgetary Survey	1970	FB	Urban New Providence	Private household within pre-established income limits	142	...	RK I	One week	E	H	65	–	Weights for index cost of living
Household Expenditure in the Bahamas	1973	FB	Nationwide	Private households	...	...	...	...	E	H	Total food	HDCxExG IxExG OxExG SExExG	–
Barbados The National Food and Nutrition Survey of Barbados	1969	N	Nationwide	Private households	700	May 69	I	...	Nc Np Nf Nv Nm	C	Total food	–	Anthropometric measurements, clinical examinations
Brazil Pesquisa sobre Consumo Alimentar	1973	N	Rio de Janeiro	Families living in certain types of dwellings	364	3 months	I DM	One week	E Nc;Np Nf;Nv Nm;Q	H C	Total food 16	I	Gini coefficient. Anthropometric measurements – Standard errors
Estudo Nacional da Despesa Familiar	1974/ 75	N FC	Nationwide	Private households	55000	One year	I DM	Seven days	Q;Nc Np;Nf Nv;Nm	O 1/	49	G	–

1/ Unit of tabulation is the "comensais-dia" (the total number of "comensais-dia" of a consumption unit, is the sum of meal attendances of the persons forming the unit during the survey week). In counting the meal attendants, the relative importance of the daily meals were also considered. The consumption unit was defined as the group of persons related by blood who share meals in the same dwelling and from the same food supply. In practice also boarders or servants, or guests, where present, were included.

Country and Title of Survey	Year of Survey	Type of Survey	Geographical coverage	Social coverage	Sample size	Duration of Survey	Method of Enumeration	Reporting period	Results Type	Results Unit	Nº of food groups/items covered	Classification & cross classification	Other results
(1)	(2)	(3)	(4)	(5)	(6)	(7)	(8)	(9)	(10)	(11)	(12)	(13)	(14)
Chile													
Encuesta de Presupuestos Familiares	1977-78	FB	...	...	...	One year	...	...	E	H	350	E S	
Colombia													
Los Presupuestos Familiares en Colombia	1971	FB	Nationwide	Private households	5404	June-July	I	8 weeks	E	H	9	GxHDC GxSE GxI	
Ingresos y Gastos de los Hogares en Colombia	1972	FB	Nationwide	Private households	2474	Sept.-Oct.	I	8 weeks	E	H	9	I HDCxG	
Dominican Rep.													
Estudio sobre Presupuestos Familiares	1969	FB FC	Santo Domingo	Private families	552	One year	I	One week	Q,Nc Np,Nf Nv,Nm	C	98	IxHDC	Consumer price index
Primera Encuesta Nacional de Ingresos y Gastos de las Familias en la Republica Dominicana	1976/77	FB	Nationwide	Private households	4457	One year	...	One week	...	...	...	...	
El Salvador													
Encuesta de Ingresos y Gastos Familiares	1969	FB	Area Metropolitana of San Salvador, four urban centres and 10 rural areas	workers and 1600[1] middle class families	One year	I	One week	E	H	212	I HDC	

1/ Data in the report refer to 446 families in San Salvador Metropolitan Area.

Country and Title of Survey	Year of Survey	Type of Survey	Geographical coverage	Social coverage	Sample size	Duration of Survey	Method of Enumeration	Reporting period	Results Type	Results Unit	No of food groups/items covered	Classification & cross classification	Other results
(1)	(2)	(3)	(4)	(5)	(6)	(7)	(8)	(9)	(10)	(11)	(12)	(13)	(14)
Guatemala													
Ingresos y Gastos de las Familias Urbanas de Guatemala	1969	FB	Cities of: Guatemala Esquintla Quetzaltenango Puerto Barrios Jutiapa	Private families of 2 persons or more	2300	One year	I	One week	E	H	17	G I HDC SE IxSE	Elasticity coefficients of demand
Guyana													
Une enquête sur la consommation des Menages dans le Department de la Guyane	1968	FB	Cayenna Kourou other coastal municipalities	Private households	93 35 50	April-June; Nov.-Dec.	RK	One week	E	H	35	G	
The National Food and Nutrition Survey of Guyana	1971	N	Nationwide	Private families and individuals	1000	April-June 1971	...	...	-	-	-	-	Recommended nutrient intakes. Child Feeding. Nutritional status of population.
Haiti													
Enquête Socio-Economique	1970	Socio-economic survey	Nationwide	Private households	...	...	...	...	E	H	Total food	G	Number of livestock, agricultural sales

Country and Title of Survey (1)	Year of Survey (2)	Type of Survey (3)	Geographical coverage (4)	Social coverage (5)	Sample size (6)	Duration of Survey (7)	Method of Enumeration (8)	Reporting period (9)	Results Type (10)	Unit (11)	Nº of food groups/items covered (12)	Classification & cross classification (13)	Other results (14)
Mexico													
Ingresos y Egresos de las Familias en la Republica Mexicana	1969–70	FB	Nationwide	Private families	...	Oct.69 ... March '70		3 days	E	H	15	I G I x G	Gini coefficients, Population statistics, Response analysis
Encuesta nacional de ingresos y gastos de los hogares	1977	FE	Nationwide	Private households	11561	One year	I	One week (recall)	E	H	Total food	I HDC G SE	
Panama													
Estudios sobre las condiciones de vida de las familias	1972	FB	Towns of: Panama Colon	Private families of 2 and more persons	1,390	One year	I	One week	E	H	15	GxI	
Peru													
Encuesta Nacional de Consumo de Alimentos	1971–72	FC FB	Nationwide	Private households	7933	One year	I	One week	E	H	...	-	
St. Lucia													
The National Food and Nutrition Survey	1974	N	Nationwide	Private households	129	Jan.-Feb.	I (Recall)	24 hours	Nc,Np Nf,Nv Nm	C	Total food		Anthropometric data
Trinidad & Tobago													
National Household Food Consumption Survey	1970	FC	Nationwide	Private households	1050	Feb.-March	RK	7 days	O,Nc Np,Nf Nv,Nm	C	12	IxHDCxG	

Country and Title of Survey	Year of Survey	Type of Survey	Geographical coverage	Social coverage	Sample size	Duration of Survey	Method of Enumeration	Reporting period	Results Type	Unit	Nº of food groups/ items covered	Classification & cross classification	Other results
(1)	(2)	(3)	(4)	(5)	(6)	(7)	(8)	(9)	(10)	(11)	(12)	(13)	(14)
Trinidad & Tobago													
Household Budgetary Survey	1971	FB	Nationwide	Private households	2800	One Year	I RK	2 weeks	E	H	41	IxG	
Household Budgetary Survey	1975/ 76	FB	Nationwide	Private households	2493	One Year	RK I	14 days	E	H	41	IxG IxHDC IxSE	

Country and Title of Survey (1)	Year of Survey (2)	Type of Survey (3)	Geographical coverage (4)	Social coverage (5)	Sample size (6)	Duration of Survey (7)	Method of Enumeration (8)	Reporting period (9)	Results Type (10)	Results Unit (11)	No of food groups/items covered (12)	Classification & cross classification (13)	Other results (14)
NEAR EAST													
Cyprus													
Household Survey	1971	FB	Nationwide	Private household	3958	One year	RK I	2 weeks	E	H	9-105	I HDC G IxG HDCxG SE SExG S SxG	
Iraq													
Household Budget and Living Conditions Survey	1971-72	FB	Nationwide	All private households	3000 each stage (3stages)	One year	I(one visit every 3-6 days)	5 weeks each stage	E Q	H C	1-10 30	G HDC E ExG	Seasonal variation study
Israel													
Family Expenditure Survey in the Administered Territories	1973/74	FB	Judaea Samaria Gaza Strip	Population in towns & refugee camps	1419	One year	RK I	2 weeks	E	H C	...	SE HDC E	
Family Expenditure Survey	1975/76	FB	Nationwide-Urban	Private families	2250	One year	RK I	One month	E Q	H Standard person	18	SE HDC E I G	

(1) Country and Title of Survey	(2) Year of Survey	(3) Type of Survey	(4) Geographical coverage	(5) Social coverage	(6) Sample size	(7) Duration of Survey	(8) Method of Enumeration	(9) Reporting period	(10) Results Type	(11) Results Unit	(12) Nº of food groups/items covered	(13) Classification & cross classification	(14) Other results
Libya													
Report on the First Phase of the Household Sample Survey	1969	FB	Tripoli town	Private households 1/	759	15.X.68 30.XI.68	I RK	One month	O 2/	–	–	I HDC IxHDC IxO	
Report on the Second Phase of the Household Sample Survey	1969	FB	Tripoli town	Private households 1/	416	1.4.69 15.5.69	I RK	One month	E	C	9	I	
Report on the First Phase of the Household Sample Survey	1969	FB	Benghazi town	Private households 1/	553	Feb.68	I RK	One month	O 2/	–	–	I HDC IxHDC IxO	
Report on the Second Phase of the Household Sample Survey	1969	FB	Benghazi Town	Private households 1/	321	May 69	I RK	One month	E	C	9	I	
Sudan													
Food Consumption Survey in Khartoum	1971	FC	Khartoum	Private families	40	June-August	I	3 days	Nc,Np Nf,Nv Nm, Q	C	Total food	–	Nutrition requirements. Health state. Anthropometric measurements
Food Consumption Survey in Soba West Village	1972	FC	Soba West Village	Private families	40	Dec.	I	3 days	Nc,Np Nf,Nv Nm	C	Total food	–	

1/ Excluding 1 person households.– 2/ Demographic and Income data.–

(1) Country and Title of Survey	(2) Year of Survey	(3) Type of Survey	(4) Geographical coverage	(5) Social coverage	(6) Sample size	(7) Duration of Survey	(8) Method of Enumeration	(9) Reporting period	(10) Results Type	(11) Unit	(12) Nº of food groups/items covered	(13) Classification & cross classification	(14) Other results
Sudan (cont'd)													
Food Consumption Survey in Jadd Hussein Village	1974	FC	Jadd Hussein Village	Private families	40	April	I	...	Nc,Np Nf,Nv Nm	C	Total food	–	) Nutrition (requirements-) Health state- (Anthropometric) measurements (
Food Intake Survey in Karan Area	1972	N	Two out of 9 villages in the area	Private families	24	Dec.	I	3 days	Q,Nc Np,Nf Nv,Nm	C	9	–	) ( ) (
Nasir Extension Food Intake Survey	...	N	Nasir	Private households	39	...	I	...	Nc Np,Nf Nv,Nm	C	Total food	–	) ( ) (
Turkey													
Nutrition in Turkey	1974	FC N	Nationwide	Private households	3533 1/	July-Sept. 1974	I	5 days	Q,Nc Np,Nf Nv,Nm	CU	18	G I HDC HDCxG IxG	Child nutrition- Anthropometric measurements- Clinical Examination

1/ Sample for the Food Consumption Survey, otherwise a total of 6480 families took part in the overall survey.-

Country and Title of Survey	Year of Survey	Type of Survey	Geographical coverage	Social coverage	Sample size	Duration of Survey	Method of Enumeration	Reporting period	Results Type	Results Unit	Nº of food groups/ items covered	Classification & cross classification	Other results
(1)	(2)	(3)	(4)	(5)	(6)	(7)	(8)	(9)	(10)	(11)	(12)	(13)	(14)
FAR EAST													
Bangladesh													
A report on the Household Expenditure Survey of Bangladesh	1973-74	FB	Nationwide	All private households	11773	One year (Quarterly Survey)	I	7 days	E Q	H	32 23	I G I x G S	
Nutrition survey of Rural Bangladesh	1975-76	FC N Dietary	Nationwide Rural - 12 locations	Private households	699	One year	I DM	2 days	Q Nc;Np Nm;Nv Nf	C	7	I	Nutritional requirements. Dietary intake Intra-family food distri-bution. Anthropometry
Hong Kong													
The Household Expenditure Survey and the Consumer Price Index	1973-74	FB	Hong Kong	Urban private households whose monthly consumption expenditure ranges from $400-$2999	2864	One year	RK I	One month	E		31	E, HDC SE E x HDC SE x E	Pricing Survey. Consumer price Indexes.
India													
All India Household Survey of Income, saving and consumer expenditure	1967-68	FB	Nationwide	Private households	4704	One year	I	One month (recall)	E	H	8	I G I x G	Elasticity of Consumer Expen-diture on selected items. Separate results for middle-class families.

Country and Title of Survey	Year of Survey	Type of Survey	Geographical coverage	Social coverage	Sample size	Duration of Survey	Method of Enumeration	Reporting period	Results Type	Results Unit	Nº of food groups/ items covered	Classification & cross classification	Other results
(1)	(2)	(3)	(4)	(5)	(6)	(7)	(8)	(9)	(10)	(11)	(12)	(13)	(14)
Indonesia													
Cost of Living Survey	1968–71	FB	Cities of: Jakarta Bandung Jogya Karta Surabaya Denpasar Medan Palembang Ujung Pandang Menado Banjamarsin Pontianak	Private households	... 807 387 842 390 375 439 436 622 496 596	One year	I RK	One week	E Q	H C	11–15	I HDC E	
National Socio-Economic Survey	1969	FB	Nationwide	Private households	...	4th round 3 months	...	...	E Q	C	11–32	E G	
National Socio-Economic Survey	1976	FB	Nationwide	Private households	...	One year	...	...	E Q	C	11–46	E G	
Japan													
Family Income and Expenditure Survey	Annual	FB	Nationwide	Excludes h/ holds engaged in agriculture forestry and fishery, and one-person households	8000	One year	RK I	6 months	E Q	H C	4–20– 209	I SE I x SE HDC; G	
National Survey of Family Income and Expenditure	1974	FB	Nationwide	Private h/ holds, excluding those engaged solely in agriculture, forestry or fishery	53000	3 months RK	3 months RK	3 months	E	H	16	G I SE HDC	Sampling errors, variation coefficients, regression coefficients.

(1) Country and Title of Survey	(2) Year of Survey	(3) Type of Survey	(4) Geographical coverage	(5) Social coverage	(6) Sample size	(7) Duration of Survey	(8) Method of Enumeration	(9) Reporting period	Results (10) Type	Results (11) Unit	(12) Nº of food groups/items covered	(13) Classification & cross classification	(14) Other results
Korea													
Report on the Results of Farm Household Economy Survey and Production Cost Survey of Agricultural Products	1972	Economic survey	Nationwide - Rural	Farm h/holds cultivating a plot of more than one "tanbo"	1200	One year	RK I	One year	Q	Farm h/hold	1	I E	Farm household economy; Production cost, Agricultural products, etc.
Annual Report 1978 on the Family Income & Expenditure Survey	1978	Economic (Annual) survey	Nationwide	Private h/holds excluding fishermen's and farmers' h/holds	4000 (ea.year)	One year	RK	One month	E	H	11	HDC; G; I; SE; I x SE; HDC x SE	
Malaysia													
Household Expenditure Survey	1973	FB	Nationwide	Private households	10943	One year	RK	One month	E	H	13	SE,E; G; SE x G; HDC; HDC x G; E x G; E x HDC	
Nepal													
Household Budget Survey	1973-75	FB	Kathmandu Lalitpur Biratnagar Bhaktapur Nepalgunj Pokhara Bhairahawa Hetauda Fana Kpur Birgunj Bhadrapur Ilan Maheudranagar Ghorahi Dhankuta Baglung Surkhet Okhaldhunga	Private households	From 288 to 672	One year	I	7 days	E	C	11	E	Evaluation of estimates

(1) Country and Title of Survey	(2) Year of Survey	(3) Type of Survey	(4) Geographical coverage	(5) Social coverage	(6) Sample size	(7) Duration of Survey	(8) Method of Enumeration	(9) Reporting period	(10) Results Type	(11) Results Unit	(12) Nº of food groups/ items covered	(13) Classification & cross classification	(14) Other results
Pakistan													
Household Income and Expenditure Survey	1968-72	FB	Urban and Rural West Pakistan	Private households	...	One year (July-June)	I	...	E Q	H C	31 21	I G I x G	
Philippines													
Food Consumption Survey 1) Luzon and Greater Manila Area	1974	FC;N	Luzon and Greater Manila Area	-	680	4 months	DM	One day	Q Nc;Np Nf;Nv Nm	C	12	-	Study of diet adequacy. Anthropometric measurements.
2) Western, Central and Eastern Visayas	1975	FC;N	Visayas	-	1503	3 months	DM	One day	Q Nc;Np Nf,Nv Nm	C	12	-	
3) Greater Manila Area	1976	FC;N	Greater Manila Area	—	459	2 months	DM	One day	Q Nc;Np Nf;Nv Nm	C	12	-	
Singapore													
Report on the Household Expenditure Survey	1972/73	FB	Nationwide	Private households	3528	One year	RK	One month	E Total food Total food	H	55	E HDC G	
Report on Survey of Households	1977	FB	Nationwide	Private households	...	Apr.-May 1977 June 1977-May 1978	...	...	...	...	...	,,,	
Sri Lanka													
Socio-Economic Survey	1969/70	FB FC	Nationwide	Private households	9694	One year	I	One week	E Q	H H;C	105	I G I x G Rounds I x Rounds	

Country and Title of Survey (1)	Year of Survey (2)	Type of Survey (3)	Geographical coverage (4)	Social coverage (5)	Sample size (6)	Duration of Survey (7)	Method of Enumeration (8)	Reporting period (9)	Results Type (10)	Unit (11)	No of food groups/ items covered (12)	Classification & cross classification (13)	Other results (14)
Sri Lanka (Contd.)													
Report on the Urban Family Budget Survey	1977	FB	7 urban centres: Colombo Dehiwala-Lavinia Kotte Kolonnawa Peliyagoda Wattala-Mabole Hendala	Private households	3200	9 weeks (1st quarter)	I	One week	E	H	18	G E E x G	
Taiwan													
Report on the Survey of Family Income and Expenditure in Taiwan	1966 (annual)	FB	Taiwan Province	Private households	400 3000	1 year 1 year	RK I	1 year 1 month	E	H	10	G x SE I x SE x G G x E G x HDC G x HDC x SE	
Thailand													
Report Socio-Economic Survey	1969	FB	Nationwide	Private households	6000	10 months	I	One month	E	H	1	I x G	
Report Socio-Economic Survey	1975-76	FB	Nationwide	Private households	9000	One year	I	One month (1 week reference for food)	E	H	14	SE x G G E x G	
Vietnam													
Family Budget Survey	1969-70	FB	Urban centres: Saigon Can-tho Dalat Nha-Trang Da-Nang	Private households	5400	One year	I	One month	E	H	14	SE x G	

(1) Country and Title of Survey	(2) Year of Survey	(3) Type of Survey	(4) Geographical coverage	(5) Social coverage	(6) Sample size	(7) Duration of Survey	(8) Method of Enumeration	(9) Reporting period	(10) Results Type	(11) Results Unit	(12) N° of food groups/items covered	(13) Classification & cross classification	(14) Other results
EUROPE													
Austria													
Food consumption	1974	FC FB	Nationwide	Private households	6674	One year	RK	One month	Q E	H,C	66	G, SE, I;E, HDC	Sampling errors
Belgium													
Household Budget Survey	1973-74	FB	Nationwide	Workers, Employees Inactive	2613	One year	RK	15 days	E	H	172	I x SE, SE x G, SE x HDC, SE x 0	
	1973-74	FB	Nationwide	Independent workers	369	One year	RK	2 weeks	E	H	172	I x SE, SE x G, SE x HDC	
Panel de Consommateurs	1975	FB	Nationwide	Private households	3346	3 months 1/	RK	14 days	E Q	C	130	I;G, SE; HDC, 0	
Denmark													
Household Budget Survey	1971	FB FC	Nationwide	Employee households	1000	One year	I RK	One month	E	H	15	I x SE, HDC x I, G x SE	Consumer credit. Real and financial wealth
Finland													
Household Survey	1971	FB FC	Nationwide	Private households	3512	One year	RK I	One month	E	H	12-294	SE x HDC, I x SE, G x HDC, HDC, G	Evaluation of emoluments in kind; Evaluation of home produce
									Q	H,C	12-204	SE, G x SE	

1/ Results refer to 3 months. The survey is a continuous marketing research

(1) Country and Title of Survey	(2) Year of Survey	(3) Type of Survey	(4) Geographical coverage	(5) Social coverage	(6) Sample size	(7) Duration of Survey	(8) Method of Enumeration	(9) Reporting period	Results		(12) N° of food groups/items covered	(13) Classification & cross classification	(14) Other results
									(10) Type	(11) Unit			
France													
Permanent Survey on Food Consumption by the French People	(Annual) 1969 1976	FC	Nationwide	Private households	10000	One year	RK I	One week	E Q E Q	C C	9-88 9-88	SE G SE G;HDC	Study of sales points. Detailed breakdown of meals taken outside home.
Germany													
Sample Survey on Income and Expenditure	1973	FB	Nationwide	All private households	52000	One year	RK I	One month	E	H	26-69	I;SE HDC I x SE I x HDC SE x HDC ...	
	1978	FB	Nationwide	All private households	22053	One year	RK I	One month	E	H	...		
Gibraltar													
Family Expenditure Survey	1972/73	FB	Nationwide	All private households	100	One year	I RK	14 days	E	H	1-35	E	
Greece													
Household Expenditure Survey	1974	FB	Nationwide	Private households	7424	...	...	...	E	H	12	E x HDC SE x E G x E	
Hungary													
Household Budget and Expenditure Survey	Annual	FB FC	Nationwide	Private households	8500	One year	RK	2 months	...	...	...	SE	

Country and Title of Survey (1)	Year of Survey (2)	Type of Survey (3)	Geographical coverage (4)	Social coverage (5)	Sample size (6)	Duration of Survey (7)	Method of Enumeration (8)	Reporting period (9)	Results Type (10)	Results Unit (11)	Nº of food groups/ items covered (12)	Classification/ & cross classification (13)	Other results (14)
Ireland Household Budget Survey	1973	FB	Nationwide	Private households	7748	One year	RK I	14 days	E	H	23– 124	G;I;HDC SE I x HDC I x SE I x G	
Household Budget Survey	1974– 77 (Annual)	FB	Nationwide – Urban areas with 1000 or more inhabitants	Private households	1396 – 1893	One year	RK I	14 days	E	H	128 52 52 52 Total food	SE I G HDC (I x HDC (I x SE (I x G	
Italy Household Consumption	Annual (latest available 1978)	FB	Nationwide	Private households	31764	One year	RK I	10 days	E Q	H	21	G x SE G x HDC SE x HDC E; G x E E x SE E x HDC	
Luxembourg Budgets Familiaux	1977	FB	Nationwide	Salaried h/holds with certain income limitations within categories: workers, employees, managers.	676	14 months	I RK	30 days	E Q	H	167 99	SE	
Norway Private Household Consumption	1973	FB	Nationwide	Private households	3363	One year	RK	2 weeks	E	H	10	I; HDC G; E	Sampling errors.

(1) Country and Title of Survey	(2) Year of Survey	(3) Type of Survey	(4) Geographical coverage	(5) Social coverage	(6) Sample size	(7) Duration of Survey	(8) Method of Enumeration	(9) Reporting period	(10) Results Type	(11) Results Unit	(12) No. of food groups/ items covered	(13) Classification & cross classification	(14) Other results
Norway (Contd.)													
Survey of Consumer Expenditure	1974–76	FB	Nationwide	Private households	3226	One year	RK I	2 weeks	E Q	H	42 10	G;E HDC; SE E x HDC E x SE	
Netherlands													
Workers Budget Enquiry	1974/75	FB	Nationwide	Workers' Families	1707	One year	RK I	One month	E	H	7	I	
Poland													
Household Budget Survey	1976	FB FC	Nationwide	4 specific groups 1/	9906	One year	RK	...	E Q	H	35	I HDC;SE	
Spain													
Family Budget Survey	1973–74	FB	Nationwide	Private households	24151	One year	I RK	7 days	E	H	13	I;G SE, HDC	Sampling errors. Analysis of non-response by 2 variables.
Sweden													
Family Expenditure Survey	1969	FB	Nationwide	Private households	4086	One year	RK	30 days	E	H	30-187	I;HDC SE;G;O I x HDC I x SE I x G I x O HDC x SE HDC x G HDC x O	

1/ Comprising wage earners and salaried employees in the socialised sector of the national economy; farmers; pensioners; and households combining farm activities with work outside agriculture.

(1) Country and Title of Survey	(2) Year of Survey	(3) Type of Survey	(4) Geographical coverage	(5) Social coverage	(6) Sample size	(7) Duration of Survey	(8) Method of Enumeration	(9) Reporting period	(10) Results Type	(11) Results Unit	(12) N° of food groups/items covered	(13) Classification & cross classification	(14) Other results
UK Family Expenditure Survey	1978 (Annual)	FB	Nationwide	Private households	10400	One year	RK I	14 days	E	H	Total food	I;HDC SE I x HDC G I x SE	Standard errors. Comparison other data available in other Govt. Departments
Household Food Consumption and Expenditure	1977	FB	Nationwide	Private households	7696	One year	RK I	One week	E;Q Nc;Np Nf;Nv Nm	H	45-150	G;I HDC I X HDC O	Nutritional value of household food. Meals out of home (special analysis). Demand analysis.
Yugoslavia Survey on Rural Households	Annual (latest available 1977)	FB FC	Nationwide	Rural	3200	One year	I	One month	E Q Nc	H Q Nc	Total food 33 Total food	G 0	Different tables for quantity of food purchased and consumed
Survey on Family Budgets of Work-ers' Households	Annual (latest available 1977)	FB	Nationwide	3 and 4 person workers' households in towns	...	One year	RK	One month	E	H	10	I HDC I x HDC	

Country and Title of Survey (1)	Year of Survey (2)	Type of Survey (3)	Geographical coverage (4)	Social coverage (5)	Sample size (6)	Duration of Survey (7)	Method of Enumeration (8)	Reporting period (9)	Results Type (10)	Results Unit (11)	No of food groups/items covered (12)	Classification & cross classification (13)	Other results (14)
NORTH AMERICA													
Canada													
Family Food Expenditure in Canada	1969	FC	Nationwide	Private households	10217	One year	RK	2 weeks	E	H	17	I; HDC G; SE G x HDC G x I	
Family Expenditure in Canada	1969	FB	Nationwide	Private households	15140	First 3 months of 1970	I	(Recall)	Q E	H H	195 Total food	G HDC;G HDC x G E; O x G SE x G; I I x G I x G x HDC	
Urban Family Food Expenditure	1974	FC	Urban cities: St John's Halifax Saint John(NB) Montreal Quebec Ottawa Toronto Thunder Bay Winnipeg Regina Saskatoon Calgary Edmonton Vancouver	Private families	14964	One year	RK	2 weeks	E Q	H H	26-93 26-93	G I HDC I x HDC G x HDC	
Urban Family Expenditure	1974	FB	"	Private families	15335	One year	I	...	E	H	1-10 [1]	0;G;HDC I;E;I x HDC E x HDC O x HDC	

[1] Detailed breakdown of meals away from home

(1) Country and Title of Survey	(2) Year of Survey	(3) Type of Survey	(4) Geographical coverage	(5) Social coverage	(6) Sample size	(7) Duration of Survey	(8) Method of Enumeration	(9) Reporting period	Results		(12) Nº of food groups/items covered	(13) Classification & cross classification	(14) Other results
									(10) Type	(11) Unit			
Canada (Contd.)													
Urban Family Food Expenditure	1976	FB	Cities of: St John's (Nfdl) Halifax Montreal Ottawa Toronto Winnipeg Edmonton Vancouver	Private families	4945	One year	RK	2 weeks	E Q	H	26–93	G I HDC I x HDC G x HDC	
Greenland													
Household Income and Expenditure Survey	1968/69	FB	Nationwide	Private households	366	...	...	...	E	H	27	I SE	
United States													
Consumer Expenditure Survey	1972–73	FB	Nationwide	Private households	23184 and 19975	Two years	RK I	2 weeks	E	H	21	I; HDC O (Housing Tenure) SE; G	
Farm Operator Family Living Expenditure	1973	FB	Nationwide	Farm Operators' families	2621	One year	I	3 visits within 12 month period	E	H	3	E	

Country and Title of Survey	Year of Survey	Type of Survey	Geographical coverage	Social coverage	Sample size	Duration of Survey	Method of Enumeration	Reporting period	Results Type	Results Unit	Nº of food groups/ items covered	Classification & cross classification	Other results
(1)	(2)	(3)	(4)	(5)	(6)	(7)	(8)	(9)	(10)	(11)	(12)	(13)	(14)
OCEANIA													
Australia													
Household Expenditure Survey	1974-75	FB	Metropolitan areas	Private households	9100	One year	I RK	2 weeks	E	H	6-39	I x G S x G HDC SE	Standard errors. Income distribution.
Fiji													
A Report on the Urban Household Income and Expenditure Survey	1972	FB	Urban centres: Suva Nausori Nadi Labasa Sigatoka Ba Lautoka	Private households	397	6 weeks	RK	2 weeks	E	H	11	I Race	
Household Income and Expenditure Survey	1973	FB	Urban centres: Suva Lautoka Nausori Ba Nadi Labasa	Private households	641	6 weeks	I	2 weeks	E	H	12	I	Income elasticities of demand and source of income by racial group.
New Caledonia													
Les budgets Familiaux en Nouvelle Caledonie	1969	FB	Nationwide	Private households	921	One year	I	1-3 weeks	E	H	37	G x Ethnic SE x Ethnic E x Ethnic x G HDC x G x Ethnic	
New Zealand													
Household Sample Survey	1973-74	FB	Nationwide	Private households	3812	One year	I	14 days	E	H	6	HDC I	
Household Survey	1974/ 75 1975/ 76 1976/ 77	FB	Nationwide	Private households	4602 2971 2847	One year	I	14 days	E	H	6	HDC I	

Country and Title of Survey	Year of Survey	Type of Survey	Geographical coverage	Social coverage	Sample size	Duration of Survey	Method of Enumeration	Reporting period	Results Type	Results Unit	Nº of food groups/ items covered	Classification & cross classification	Other results
(1)	(2)	(3)	(4)	(5)	(6)	(7)	(8)	(9)	(10)	(11)	(12)	(13)	(14)
Papua New Guinea													
Household Expenditure Survey	1975-76	FB	Six urban centres: Port Moresby Lae Kieta/Avana/ Pauguna Rabaul Goroka Madang	Papua New Guinean's Private households	176	One year	I	2 weeks	E	H	-	HDC	
Western Samoa													
Survey of Households' Living Conditions in Western Samoa	1971/72	FB	Nationwide	Private households	333	Aug.'71-Jan.'72	I RK	One week	E	H	10	I G HDC	